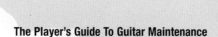

The Player's Guide To Guitar Maintenance
A practical manual to get the most from your electric guitar
By Dave Burrluck

A BALAFON BOOK
First edition 1998

Published in the United States by Miller Freeman Books, 600 Harrison Street, San Francisco, CA 94107.
Publishers of Guitar Player and Bass Player magazines.
Miller Freeman, Inc. is a United News and Media company.

Published and originated in the UK by Balafon Books, an imprint of Outline Press Ltd,
115J Cleveland Street, London W1P 5PN, England.

ISBN 0-87930-549-5

Printed in Hong Kong

Art Director: Nigel Osborne
Design: Sally Stockwell
Editor: Tony Bacon
Technical Consultant: Bill Puplett
Photography: Miki Slingsby
Production: Phil Richardson

Print and origination by Regent Publishing Services

98 99 00 01 02 5 4 3 2 1

To make the best music you need every bit of help you can get. This book won't make you play better, but aims to improve the condition and maximise the efficiency of your musical tool, the electric guitar. The help you'll find in here bridges the gap between the usually scant info you'll get in an owner's guide and the tech-heavy repair manuals for the wannabe professional repairer or maker.

An old guitar that's been gigged for years might require quite serious repair, but many new guitars – especially lower-priced ones – can be vastly improved by the relatively simple steps described in this book.

If the thought of picking up a screwdriver has previously scared you, don't worry. We'll guide you through even the most basic adjustments, and equally we'll tell you when to stop and seek professional advice.

We'll explain your guitar's electric components, show you how to string it up and adjust its neck, bridge and vibrato. And along the way you'll learn about the history and technical development of one of the most expressive musical instruments ever created.

In this book we will be offering a series of techniques and tips that will help you get the very best from your electric guitar. Inside the book you will discover four main sections called Strings, Neck, Bridge/Vibrato, and Electrics, as well as a couple of mini-sections that deal with tools and suggest cleaning tips.

But first, before we get into the main portion of the book, on these three pages here you'll find quick and simple clarifications of the general terms and names used for the various parts of electric guitars. (You will probably also find it useful from time to time to consult the more detailed Glossary that is located toward the back of this book.)

We've concentrated on the two main designs of solidbody guitar that continue to dominate the music industry, namely Fender's Stratocaster and Gibson's Les Paul, and it is these two designs that we have illustrated and described here. Do bear in mind, however, that we have during the course of the book also included a number of other popular designs of electric guitars and guitar hardware, wherever they are appropriate and useful. Most of the work in the book is carried out on the Fender Strat and Epiphone Les Paul guitars shown in detail here. But many of the design features of these two instruments and the terms used for them are the same as or similar to those of a large number of other brands and models.

Once you have familiarised yourself with the terms and names here, we invite you to join us on the following nine pages – before the main portion of the book starts – for a concise tour of the electric guitar's history. This is designed as an informative guide to the broad variety of electric guitars (to which the general terms and names discussed here also apply, of course).

Welcome to *The Player's Guide To Guitar Maintenance*. We trust that it will serve you well and increase your understanding of your chosen instrument.

*The Strat's **headstock** (above) contains six **tuners**, or "machine heads", used to keep the strings in tune. This guitar also has a **string tree**, to increase the behind-the-nut angle of the two highest strings.*

*In contrast to the simple style of the original Fender solidbody guitars, Gibson's Les Paul was more decorative, for example using edge **binding** on the body and the fingerboard (below).*

*The **backplates** on the rear of the Les Paul's body (left) are removed here to reveal the toggle switch and associated wiring (right), as well as the control **pots** and wiring (left).*

*The **truss-rod cover** on the headstock (below) reveals access to the truss-rod adjuster.*

*Many Gibson-style guitars have 22 **frets**, like this Epiphone Les Paul. **Position markers** on this example are Gibson "crown" types. Vintage-style Fenders usually have 21 frets, like the Strat opposite, but many modern Fenders have 22.*

*The Les Paul's **neck** is glued to the body. You will also hear this referred to as a "set neck" or "fixed neck" construction.*

*Les Paul-style guitars usually have their six **tuners** (machine heads) in two groups of three on either side of the headstock, as on this Epiphone (above).*

Pickups are at the heart of an electric guitar. They convert one form of energy – a vibrating string – into another – an electrical signal that can be amplified. On the earliest solidbody electric, Fender adapted their existing lap-steel pickup for the Telecaster's bridge pickup (right), the angled position accentuating treble. Bridges on original Teles (1953 example below, with cover) and vintage-style Teles (1997 example, right) have three saddles.

1953 Fender Telecaster

Rickenbacker were responsible for quite a few significant innovations at the early stages of the development of the electric guitar, not least their introduction of the first electric guitar fitted with an electro-magnetic pickup. By the mid 1950s, when the Combo 400 model with "through-neck" construction was launched (right), Rickenbacker shared the solidbody electric guitar market in the US with a number of other important makers such as Fender, Gibson, Kay, Harmony and Gretsch.

The first electric guitars began to appear during the 1930s, and were mostly either hollow-body instruments converted for amplified use by the addition of crude, early pickups, or lap-steel guitars for Hawaiian-style playing. But it wasn't until the 1950s that the solidbody electric guitar really began to make its mark as a modern instrument with an important voice, specifically with the arrival on to the market of Fender's first "Spanish electric" guitars.

Back then, most guitarists wanted louder instruments so that they would be heard in the midst of the busy sound generated by a large group in a dancehall. Acoustic instruments just did not have the carrying power.

Rickenbacker had been the first company to use an electro-magnetic pickup on a guitar, in the early 1930s, when the term "Spanish" began to be used for the normal (but then less popular) non-lap steel guitar. Rickenbacker

were also innovative in selling hollow-body electric guitars then, along with National, Gibson and Epiphone. At first the impact of these instruments was small, although later such fine guitars as Gibson's ES-175 (1949) and L-5CES (1951) would set high standards among modern hollow-body electrics.

Some guitar makers and musicians began to think about the possibility of a solidbody instrument. It would be without the annoying feedback often produced by amplified hollow-body guitars, and allow louder playing. It would also be cheaper to produce. Rickenbacker issued a relatively solid Bakelite-body electric guitar in the mid 1930s, while around 1940 guitarist Les Paul built a personal test-bed electric guitar with a solid central block of pine.

Paul Bigsby in California made some distinctive early solidbody guitars, starting in 1948 with the historic Merle Travis "through-neck" guitar. Also in California, Leo Fender had

begun in the music business in the mid 1940s, making electric lap-steel guitars and amplifiers. The small Fender company started work in the summer of 1949 on the instrument which we know today as the Fender Telecaster, effectively the world's first commercially-marketed solidbody electric guitar. It was first produced by Fender during 1950, initially as the Fender Esquire, then as the Broadcaster, and finally as the Telecaster.

The design is still, of course, very much alive today, and continues to embody the elements that attracted Leo Fender and his early customers: ease of construction, simplicity of design, and a cutting, clean sound. Despite apparent refinements and developments by Fender and all manner of other makers, players can still enjoy the Telecaster not only for what it is – a great guitar – but as a way of connecting with the earliest days of the solidbody electric guitar.

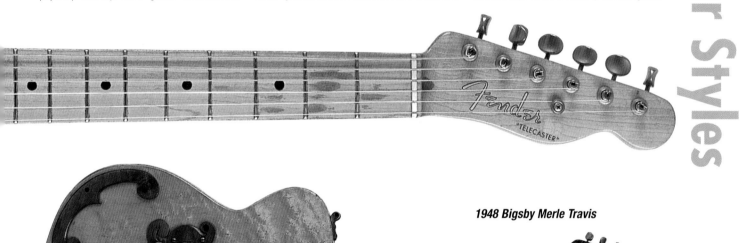

1948 Bigsby Merle Travis

1956 Rickenbacker Combo 400

The first solidbody electric guitar to have a notable commercial impact was the Fender Telecaster. But before Fender's historic 1950 launch there were earlier experiments, many of which were too far ahead of their time to have any real effect. Paul Bigsby is best known for the vibrato unit that bears his name, but in the late 1940s, in collaboration with country guitarist Merle Travis, he custom-built one of the earliest solidbody electric guitars (above), with a design that

looks remarkably modern. There can be little doubt that this guitar, made about 15 miles from Leo Fender's workshop, had a direct influence on Fender's later solidbody electric guitar designs, not least the headstock shape of the Stratocaster. A major difference between the Bigsby and Fenders is Bigsby's "through-neck", where the neck extends right through the entire length of the instrument. Bigsby probably applied the idea as a result of the way he built steel guitars.

Electric Guitar Styles

The Les Paul is Gibson's leading solidbody electric guitar. Although first introduced in 1952, it was the later Sunburst version (below), originally made only between 1958 and 1960, that is regarded as the finest flowering of the Les Paul design. This version has since been the subject of many vintage-style reissues and modern updates. The Sunburst features Gibson's classic humbucking pickups, an example of which is shown (left) without its cover, revealing the unit's twin coils.

The first Les Paul of 1952 was the original Gold-top model (below) with "trapeze" tailpiece and P90 pickups. Subsequent changes led to the late-1950s Gold-top (bottom) with Tune-o-Matic bridge and humbucking pickups.

1952 Gibson Les Paul "Gold-top"

1958 Gibson Les Paul "Gold-top"

Gibson's Les Paul design came about in the early 1950s as a reaction to Fender's recently introduced solidbody electric guitar. Gibson had been producing guitars for much, much longer than the upstart Fender, and Gibson's version of the new solidbody style reflected the company's traditional view of guitar making, although in itself the Gibson Les Paul was as revolutionary as Fender's Telecaster.

Gibson released their first Les Paul model, since nicknamed the Gold-top thanks to its coloured finish, during 1952. Gibson were smart enough to have their new design endorsed by Les Paul, the most popular electric guitarist in America at the time thanks to his guitar-laden hit records (including 'How High The Moon' with vocalist Mary Ford). Where the Fender was being made with a

simple, bolt-together construction, Gibson's Les Paul was more refined, with a carved maple cap on a mahogany body, ornate fingerboard inlays, neck and body binding, and a raised pickguard.

Some of the constructional differences contributed to a different sound, too. But when in the later 1950s Gibson added their new humbucking pickups to the Les Paul, a distinct contrast was evident when compared to the sound of the single-coil pickups that were fitted to all Fender electric guitars at the time. Single-coils then were generally bright and cutting, while humbuckers were usually more powerful and warmer sounding.

A number of variations on the original Les Paul model have appeared from Gibson since 1952, some merely cosmetic, others more

fundamental, and we have shown the major types on these pages. Not illustrated is the Les Paul Custom, a black-finish variant that often features three humbuckers and first appeared in 1954.

Gibson completely redesigned the Les Paul models in 1961, opting for a "modern" double-cutaway design (now known as the SG style) in an attempt to increase sales. But after musicians such as Eric Clapton started playing the old-style Les Pauls in the 1960s, Gibson were forced to reintroduce the original-design Les Paul models in 1968.

Like Fender's two classic designs, the Telecaster and the Stratocaster, most of Gibson's various Les Paul models are still very much in evidence today, underlining the timelessness of the original designs.

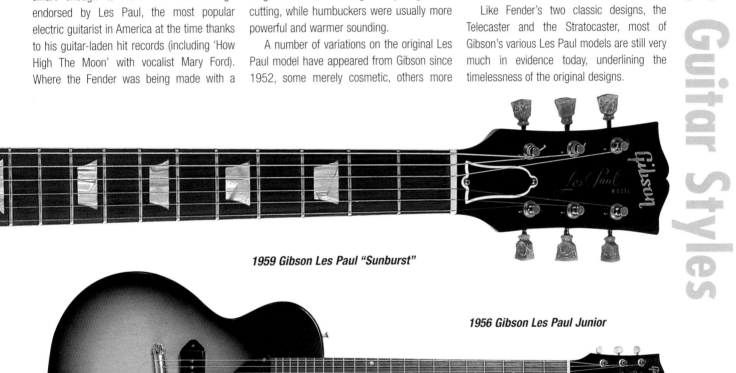

1959 Gibson Les Paul "Sunburst"

1956 Gibson Les Paul Junior

Gibson first issued their cheaper Junior and Special versions of the Les Paul in the mid 1950s, with non-carved body tops and simpler features. The Junior (above) had a single P90 pickup, while the Special (below) had two. At first they came with a single-cutaway shape (above), but in the late 1950s the bodies were revised to a double-cutaway style (below).

1959 Gibson Les Paul Special

The Stratocaster started life looking exactly like this pristine 1956 example (below), and such early vintage Strats form the basis of many collections as well as Fender's reissue lines. One of the key features of the original design was the Strat's fully adjustable bridge (shown left, without cover). Many versions and copies and developments of the Strat have followed since the 1950s launch, not least with Fender's own successful update in 1986, the American Standard Stratocaster.

1956 Fender Stratocaster

The Superstrat of the 1980s (Jackson, below) was Strat-inspired but with 24 frets, a humbucker/single-coil mix, locking vibrato and pointed headstock. It was aimed at a new breed of fast-fingered, high-volume players personified by Eddie Van Halen and Steve Vai.

1990 Jackson Soloist

The Fender Stratocaster first appeared in 1954. It can be seen as a reaction by Fender to Gibson's Les Paul, as Fender's attempt to produce a fancier and more refined guitar than their ground-breaking Telecaster.

The Strat is still a striking guitar today... but just imagine how it must have looked to guitarists when it first appeared more than 40 years ago. It has of course since become the most celebrated, the most fashionable and the most *played* electric guitar of all time, a staple of every kind of popular music and an icon of 1950s design.

It is also a very good musical instrument, and benefits once again from the clean simplicity which had endowed its older cousin, the Telecaster, with such efficiency – but this time with an added dash of style and elegance.

The Strat literally rounded the Tele's hard outlines, added a second cutaway for upper-fret access, and was the first solidbody electric with three pickups. It also had a brilliantly designed vibrato – an adjustable bridge, a tailpiece and a vibrato system, all in one unit – and featured a radically sleek, solid body, contoured for the player's comfort.

We have now met the three solidbody electric guitar designs that still dominate the thoughts of guitar players and guitar makers: the Fender Telecaster, the Gibson Les Paul and the Fender Stratocaster, although of course there have been many other brands, models and further developments since those three original and inimitable 1950s designs.

Gibson dabbled with adventurous body shapes during the late 1950s with the Explorer and the Flying V, settling down briefly with the SG and the Firebird in the 1960s, while Fender added the new Jazzmaster and Jaguar to their line. In the 1970s Japanese companies began to prove that they could build good solidbody electric guitars, including Yamaha's SG line, while smaller US companies such as Hamer, Dean and B.C Rich began to exploit the poor reputation of many of the contemporary Gibson and Fender products. Also at this time, DiMarzio started the retrofit craze.

In the 1980s the Strat-style vibrato was given a modern facelift by Floyd Rose, the Strat design was reinterpreted by US companies Kramer and Jackson along with Japanese outfit Ibanez, and a smart revision of the best of Fender and Gibson ideas resulted in Paul Reed Smith's new PRS guitars.

The 1990s was a decade of extremes: from "retro" fever that lauded everything vintage or vintage-style, to the ultra-modern build and electrics of the Parker Fly. Let's hope that the next five decades of the solidbody electric guitar are at least as exciting.

1959 Epiphone Crestwood

Fender was not alone in influencing other guitar makers. Gibson bought Epiphone in the 1950s (when this Crestwood, above, was made). Gretsch too was never far behind the changes made to Gibson guitars, although Gretsch's distinctive sparkle-front finishes (below) were all their own.

1955 Gretsch Silver Jet

Gibson's 335, as well as many other of the company's models, was fitted as standard with a Tune-o-Matic bridge and stop tailpiece (as on this 1959 example, left). At this time some Gibson electrics were fitted at the factory with Bigsby vibratos, and for 335-type guitars this meant that the holes already drilled for the normal stop tailpiece would have to be filled. This was done either with pearl dots (as seen on the example below), or with a black plate inscribed "Custom Made".

1960 Gibson ES-335

Rickenbacker popularised the idea of the 12-string electric guitar in the 1960s with their distinctive American-made guitars (below). The lower four pairs of strings are tuned an octave apart and the highest two in unison to create a rich, ringing, jangling sound.

For an explanation of the general tools pictured above, please consult the numbered key at the top of the right-hand page .

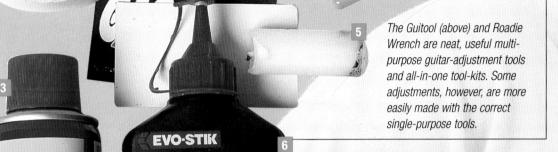

The Guitool (above) and Roadie Wrench are neat, useful multi-purpose guitar-adjustment tools and all-in-one tool-kits. Some adjustments, however, are more easily made with the correct single-purpose tools.

TOOLS & MATERIALS

Most of the tools you'll need will be available from a good hardware and/or electrical store.

Your basic equipment must include an accurate steel ruler (and ideally a set of feeler gauges) for general measurements.

Screwdrivers are essential, especially cross-head types, and you'll need a small, medium and large size. Small and medium size flat-blade screwdrivers will serve most other applications. It's worth bearing in mind that you should *not* undo or tighten a cross-head screw with a flat-blade screwdriver.

A small collection of Allen keys is also essential. Most new guitars come with the correct size Allen keys for truss-rod and bridge. Keep these safe. US-made hardware invariably uses imperial size Allen keys; European-made and Far Eastern-made parts (from Japan and Korea, for example) invariably use metric sizes. To adjust the saddle heights on a Japanese-made reissue Strat, for example, you'll need a 1.5mm Allen key; to adjust the same on a US-made American Standard Strat you'll need a slightly smaller .050″ or marginally smaller ³⁄₆₄″ key.

Imperial-size keys of .050″, ¹⁄₁₆″, ⁵⁄₆₄″, ³⁄₃₂″ and ⁵⁄₃₂″ and metric-size keys of 1.5mm, 2.5mm, 3mm and 3.5mm will get regular use on most types of bridges and vibratos. Truss-rod adjustments are made with either a larger Allen key, around the ³⁄₁₆″ to 7mm sizes, or a supplied socket-head nut wrench typically either ¼″ or ⁵⁄₁₆″.

HANDY MATERIALS

1 Masking tape
2 Soft pencil for nut-slot lubrication
3 Penetrating oil
4 Card for neck shims
5 Candle wax for screw lubrication
6 Wood adhesive
7 Wood veneer for neck shims
8 Capo
9 Contact- and switch-cleaner

Gibson's ES-335 model, introduced in 1958, unveiled a new kind of electric guitar. It was in effect a cross between a solidbody and a hollow-body instrument.

As we've already discovered, some of the earliest electric guitars were hollow-body types. While these had gradually found a ready market, especially among jazz players, other guitarists who wanted to play louder had little choice but to play a solidbody style of electric. However, some still yearned for the acoustic tones of a hollow-body instrument.

That was when Gibson's designers decided to try to combine the quality of a hollow-body guitar with the high-volume capability of a solidbody. The result was the 335, which was really a development of Gibson's thin-body "thinline" design that had begun with models

such as the Byrdland and the ES-350T a few years earlier in the mid 1950s.

With the 335, however, Gibson not only introduced a radical double-cutaway body, but also employed a novel solid wooden block running through the centre of the body from neck to tailpiece, thus creating a new "semi-solid" structure. (Many players often refer to any thin, hollow-body electric – whether or not it has a centre block – as a "semi".)

Gibson's idea was effectively to combine a hollow-body guitar with a solidbody, not only in terms of construction but also in sonic effect. The 335's solid maple block (inside what Gibson described as its "wonder-thin" body) quelled the feedback so often heard from loud hollow-body guitars, and was intended to offer a new combination of pure solidbody sustain

with the pleasing warmth usually associated with a hollow-body instrument.

Of course, some rock players do use fully hollow-body electric guitars to great effect, some turning feedback from a nuisance into a creative event, others simply by playing at quieter levels. A couple of examples from Rickenbacker and Gretsch are shown here, and many other brands and models have appeared over the years.

Gibson developed the 335 design for more models, including the ES-345 and ES-355 of 1959 which also feature stereo wiring and an unusual Varitone preset tone switch. But it is the 335 that remains the classic semi-solid electric guitar, and one that like the Tele, Strat and Les Paul will probably continue to be played well into the 21st century.

1966 Gretsch White Falcon Stereo

Gretsch guitars are known for their unusual and stylish looks. The company pioneered the coloured paint finish, borrowing two-tone effects and sparkle plastics from their drum department, resulting in classics like the White Falcon. By the time this example appeared Gretsch's love of gadgetry was in full swing: this one has angled high frets supposedly to improve intonation, a "Floating Sound" frame-style bridge, twin string dampers, and a multiple stereo control layout.

1964 Rickenbacker 330S/12-1993

GENERAL TOOLS
10 Feeler gauge
11 6″ steel rule
12 Box spanners
13 Heavy-duty cutters
14 Pliers with taped jaws
15 Floyd Rose intonation adjuster
16 Truss-rod socket-head nut wrenches

17 Various Allen keys
18 Stewart-MacDonald radius gauges
19 Wire-cutters
20 String-winder
21 Cross-head screwdrivers
22 Flat-blade screwdrivers
23 Seymour Duncan combined cross-
   head and flat-blade screwdriver

SOLDERING EQUIPMENT
24 De-soldering gun (solder sucker)
25 Multicore solder
26 Wire strippers
27 Wire-cutters
28 Soldering iron stand
29 Soldering iron

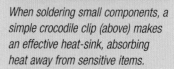

Use a multimeter (above) for checks such as electrical continuity. It's not essential, but could be useful if you get into more complex guitar repairs.

When soldering small components, a simple crocodile clip (above) makes an effective heat-sink, absorbing heat away from sensitive items.

Some simple adjustments like tightening/ loosening the circular retaining nut on a Les Paul-style toggle switch can be difficult without the use of the proper tool (Toggle Switch Wrench pictured; see p66 for more information).

Specialist tools are not essential for the work in this book, but to safely carry out some adjustments pro tools like Stewart-MacDonald's Stop Tailpiece Post wrench ❶ and their Toggle Switch wrench ❷ are worth considering. For basic nut and fret work you need a special razor saw ❸ and various files ❹ ❺, and for fitting new tuners you need a peg-hole reamer ❻ that'll cost as much as the new tuners. For these reasons, plus the fact that work on the nut and frets requires a lot of skill, such areas are not featured in this book. General tools like a set of needle files ❼ are handy though not essential, and a drill bit ❽ and hand drill ❾ are necessary for adding a mini-toggle switch (see p76).

Protect your work-surface with a piece of carpet or blanket, with newspapers, or with non-slip rubber such as this specially designed Guitar Maintenance System mat (below).

WORKING ENVIRONMENT

It's well worth considering your working environment before you attempt even the most basic adjustment techniques described in this book. All you need is a firm table or work-surface in an uncluttered, well-lit area.

Always protect the table with a blanket or newspapers or a non-slip rubber mat. The Guitar Maintenance System, as pictured (left), is a neat non-slip mat and neck support that's handy but not essential. A neck support is very useful; in fact, any solid block protected with cloth will suffice.

Always keep tools away from your main working area and wherever possible protect the finish of your guitar with a cloth or duster, especially when soldering. Always put screws and other tiny parts in a small container so that they don't get lost or damage your guitar.

A quiet, calm environment is essential so you can concentrate: distractions like young children and family pets should be removed.

Wear safety glasses when soldering and snipping wires or strings, and never leave tools or string-ends around – they are dangerous.

Always double-check that you've switched off and unplugged your soldering iron, and leave plenty of time for it to cool down before your pack it away.

The majority of tools, materials and parts that you'll need are available from good hardware stores, even music stores. But finding a good all-in-one supplier is worthwhile. Stewart-MacDonald's Guitar Shop Supply based in the US [fax: +1 (406) 586-1030] have a huge catalogue (left) of tools, parts, books and kits for amateurs and pros alike. In the UK, Kent Armstrong's Rainbow Products [tel: +44 (0)123373-2527] supply WD guitar parts and accessories (catalogue, left), and specialise in pickup rewinds, potting and one-off designs. Of course, these aren't the only specialist companies: check out the ads and send off for a variety of catalogues and pricelists.

STRING TYPES

You've probably given a lot of thought to the type and style of guitar you want and struggled to find the money to buy it.

But have you ever given a thought to the strings you're going to use, or how frequently you should change them? Let's face it, the type of strings you use on your guitar and their general condition will form the starting point of good guitar tone.

In reality we're spoilt for choice, though you need to bear in mind that the majority of string brands are produced by just a few string manufacturers. In fact, you should try to choose the strings you use based on their consistency and their availability.

The most common type of strings for electric guitar are "nickel" roundwounds. What that means is that the wound strings – typically the three low strings – have nickel-plated steel windings (wraps) around a steel core. The unwound strings – typically the top three – are plain steel.

A small metal "ball" is wound onto each string at one end – this is the "ball-end" that serves to secure the string into the anchor point at the bridge. You'll need to cut this off before you can use a string for a Floyd Rose vibrato (see Bridge/Vibrato: general tips p5?). Some special strings do come already without ball-ends for this purpose.

You'll also see "stainless steel" strings. D'Addario introduced this type back in the mid 1970s, and they now use "400-series magnetic stainless steel" instead of nickel-plated steel wraps. D'Addario use this material on their flatwound Chromes (where a flat-section outer winding is used). They also use it for their Half Round strings (where the oversized stainless steel winding is partially ground down to offer some of the smoothness of flatwound strings) which offer reduced finger-noise and less fret wear, but with some of the brightness of roundwounds.

Stainless steel strings typically sound a little brighter initially, but become duller more quickly than nickel. Nickel strings usually sound slightly more mellow, but tend to die less quickly.

Do bear in mind that these are generalisations, and that you're advised to experiment with different strings. However, when you do experiment, it's more useful to compare the different winding types of the *same* brand and the *same* gauge.

STRING LOADING I: BASIC

Being able to change your strings efficiently is the first stage of guitar maintenance. There are many ways to attach the strings to the tuners. You need to establish your own working practice, one that secures the strings efficiently and suits your own guitar and the style you play in. Here's a basic method.

1 Lay your guitar on your worktop in front of you with the headstock (supported if it's back-angled) to your left or whichever way is most comfortable. Unless you need to clean your fingerboard, or do any other maintenance or modification, always replace your strings one at a time. Use a string winder to quickly slacken the string and remove it from the tuner's string-post – start with the low E-string. Remember that the plain end of the string was probably cut to length with wire-cutters and will be extremely sharp, so watch your fingers, eyes and guitar finish. Remove the old string from the bridge and discard it. Set the tuner so that the hole in its string-post (diagram A above) is parallel to the nut. Thread the new string through the tailpiece or bridge and carefully pull it down to the tuner's string-post. Place the string against the inside edge of the post and pull it tightly (pictured).

2 Now wind the string around the string-post anti-clockwise (counter-clockwise) for one full turn (see diagram B above), keeping the tension on, and thread it through the string-post hole (diagram C above). This will add another turn *above* the first (pictured).

A   **B**   **C**

3 Pull the string out of the other side of the string-post hole and pull it as tight as you can. Bend the loose end of the string at a right angle and slightly downwards immediately at the point it emerges from the string-post hole. Tune up to pitch. Repeat this procedure for the A-string and D-string. If you have a six-a-side headstock, use the same technique for *all* strings; if you have a three-a-side headstock the procedure is the same except it becomes a mirror image for the second set of three tuners which are mounted on the opposite side of the headstock. Now wind on your plain strings. Whereas you have ended up with just a couple of turns around the string-post on the wound strings, the plain strings need a few more turns. Wrap the string neatly around the string-post three or four times before poking the lose end through the string-post hole. Stretch your strings (see later in this section, p23), tune the strings up to pitch, and then check that your intonation is accurate and reset it if necessary (see Bridge/Vibrato: intonation, p48-49).

Finally, clip the loose end of the string a few millimetres away from the post (see final attachment pictured). Some players like to curl the loose string in a circle, which is fine – but never leave the loose ends hanging, because they can be dangerous.

BASIC STRING LOADING

 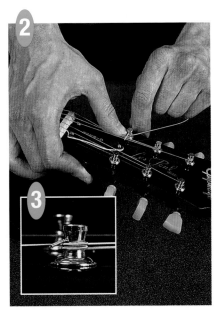

STRING LOADING II: LOCKING

Many players and repairmen prefer to lock the string around the tuner's string-post for additional security and tuning stability, and it makes sense to do this if you have a vibrato (without a locking nut or locking tuners). This method requires a little more dexterity and, because of the lock, it may not be quite as quick to remove the strings – something to consider if you break a string on-stage and you haven't got your own guitar tech. However, practice makes perfect.

1 Start off exactly the same as the basic method (left) but this time turn the tuner's string-post so that the hole is approximately 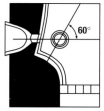 60 degrees to the nut (see diagram here). With your left hand, pull the string to the inside edge of the string-post but hold it with your right hand to create some slack length (as pictured below). Holding the string firm at the tuner with your left hand, move your right hand down the string to the tuner, and grip the string. (Alternatively you could poke the string through the string-post first and then estimate your slack, but you must be very careful not to bend the string in the wrong place.)

2 Poke the loose end through the string-post hole from the centre of the headstock outwards (see diagram D above). Pull the loose end through the hole but don't lose the grip on your right hand because that's still creating the slack. Bend the loose end clockwise around the post (see diagram E below) and under the point where the string is entering the post (see diagram F below). Hold the string momentarily with the first finger of your right hand, then grab the loose end again with your left hand and pull it tightly as you bend it upwards and over the string (see picture at bottom of page).

D   **E**   **F**

3 Hold the string in place with your right-hand thumb and tighten the tuner so that the "speaking length" of the string clamps the loose end tightly (the speaking length is the portion that goes from the tuner, over the nut, and on to the bridge). Then, with your string winder in your left hand, carefully wind on the slack, making neat turns *below* the first turn. If you've estimated your slack correctly you should get approximately two to three turns. Again, if your guitar has a three-a-side headstock, the procedure on the treble strings is a mirror image. Having attached, tuned, and stretched all your strings, and if necessary re-set your intonation, make a final downward bend where the loose end of each string emerges from the post, and clip off the string as close as you can to the post (see finished attachment pictured).

ALTERNATIVE LOCKS

Follow the locking procedure described (left) to the point where you start winding on the slack in step three. Now, instead of your first wind going under the locked string, try one over and the remaining turns under. For extra security, you could try two over and the remainder under. Whatever locking method you use, be flexible. If your tuner has a short string-post, it will not be practical to use a double-locking method, especially if you are using heavy gauge strings (see Golden Rules, p23).

Locking tuners take the guess-work out of string loading. For example, Sperzel's Trim-Loks (below), require that you simply thread the string through the string-post hole, pull it tight, tighten the lock on the back of the tuner housing, and tune up. One thing to remember with any locking tuners is that you must always fully slacken the string before undoing the lock. Don't undo the lock with the string tuned to pitch.

LOCKING STRING LOADING

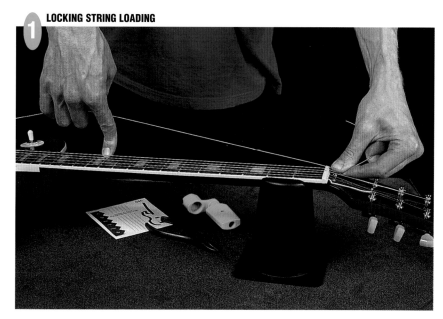

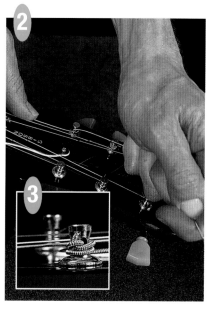

STRING LOADING III: SLOT-HEAD TUNERS

Vintage Fenders and the numerous modern reissues often use slot-head vintage-style tuners (or "SafetiPost" tuners). While you can use the methods on p20/21 – the slot is just like an open-topped string-post hole – slot-head tuners were originally designed so that the loose end of the string is placed down the hole in the centre of the post. This tidy method never leaves any sharp string-ends protruding. Remember to replace the strings *one at a time*. If you have a vibrato and need to remove all the strings at once, place the backplate, or a stack of business cards, under the back edge of the vibrato *before* you remove the strings.

1 Lay the guitar in front of you, remove the old string, and set the tuner slot so it's parallel with the nut. Load the new string through the bridge. Pull it tight against the inside of the tuner's string-post. You need to allow approximately the distance of two tuners (50mm/2") for winding on (see Headstock Angles, right), so if you're fitting the low E-string, make a right-angled bend in the string at a point coinciding with the D-string tuner. Cut the string to length approximately 10mm (⅜") beyond the right-angled bend (pictured).

2 Poke the loose end of the string down, as far as it will go, into the central hole in the tuner's string-post, and then hold the string down into the bottom of the slot (pictured).

3 Hold the string in place with your right-hand thumb while, with your string winder in your left hand (pictured), you tighten the tuner, making sure that the slack string is neatly wound down the post.

4 The finished string attachment is shown in this final picture.

STRING LOADING WITH SLOT-HEAD TUNERS

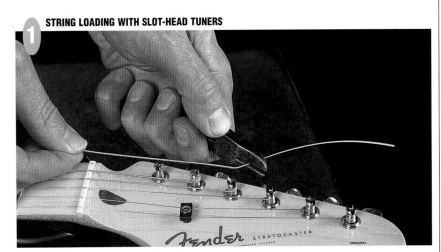

HEADSTOCK ANGLES

The type of headstock you have will affect the way in which you need to load your strings. This is because the angle at which the string "breaks" from the nut to the tuners plays a part in the tone of your guitar and its tuning stability. If the string angle is too shallow, the string can rattle in the nut slot and cause a loss of tone and, at worst, a sitar-like buzz. On guitars with a standard back-angled headstock (without a locking nut) you need to aim for around two to four neat string turns around the tuner's string-post. Clearly this depends on the gauge of the string and the height of the string-post hole above the tuner bushing. For example, a heavy gauge low E-string on a short string-post will require fewer turns than a lighter-gauge E-string on a longer post.

On Fender-style straight headstocks you need to be a little more clever, especially when you only have one string tree on the top two strings. On the low E-string, aim for two turns (too many here will create too steep an angle which may impair tuning stability, especially if you have a vibrato). On the A-string aim for two to three turns; the D-string needs about four turns. The G-string is the most problematic, and you need as many turns as you can down the string-post, almost to the turner bushing itself. This will create the maximum behind-the-nut string angle. Because the top two strings, B and E, pass under the string tree(s), they need only four turns or so.

Obviously, the more turns you require, the more slack you need to allow (or the longer the string-length must be before you cut it off). It takes some experience to estimate these turns, especially with slot-head tuners.

Some locking tuners help the problem, especially on Fender-style headstocks, as they have "staggered-height" string-posts to help you achieve the correct behind-the-nut string angle. Gotoh have recently introduced their HAP locking tuners which allow you precisely to set the height of each individual tuner post.

STRING STRETCHING

Without getting too scientific, we can consider a string as having three stages in its life-cycle. When you first load new strings they are extremely elastic and sound very bright and "fresh". Until they settle, however, they won't stay in tune. Once you've stretched them and played them in – the second phase – they're at their optimum. How long they stay like this is down to numerous factors: primarily how much and how aggressively you play, and how much you sweat.

The combination of playing, your sweat, and the dirt that will accumulate on the strings will lead to the final stage of their life: the strings becoming "dead". This is where they lose their tonal brightness and physical elasticity, making them much more prone to breakage, especially at the tuners and saddles where they are in contact with metal.

You can prolong the life of the strings by wiping them, with a cloth or a string cleaner, after every playing session. But you can't alter the physical decay due to playing wear. Any new strings must be stretched. Players will use their own different techniques for this, but the aim is always the same: to make sure they settle and, therefore, stay in tune. Here's a basic method.

• First, grip a string somewhere near the pickups and lightly pull it away from the guitar. Do this to each string in turn. This will relieve any hitching at the tuners, nut and bridge.
• Lay the guitar in front of you and grip and squeeze each string with your left-hand thumb and fingers, moving along the entire length of the string. Then bend each string a few times behind the nut and, if relevant, behind the bridge. I find that holding the string over the bridge saddle with your right-hand thumb will stop any unnecessary friction-wear which could lead – especially on the lighter strings – to premature breakage. Stretch each string one at a time, constantly re-checking your tuning as you go. When the string no longer de-tunes after some pretty heavy bending, the string is stretched. String-stretching is a balance between getting your new strings to settle in tune, but not over-stretching them to such an extent that the windings around the core distort and impair your tone.

TUNING TIPS

The availability of the accurate, low-cost electronic tuner makes getting your guitar in tune, and setting its intonation, straightforward. (Just to clarify: by "electronic tuner" we mean the typically battery-powered device that you tune your guitar to.) If you haven't got an electronic tuner you'll need some kind of reference – for example from a keyboard, pitch pipe or tuning fork. Tune the low E-string first, pluck an open string or 12th-fret harmonic, and always tune *up* to pitch from a *flat* note. If the string is already sharp, drop it down below the correct pitch and then bring it back up.

Tuning is always a compromise, thanks to the combination of numerous factors such as the string's initial elasticity and the condition of your guitar's tuners, nut, bridge, strings and frets. The compromise is furthered by the way in which the actual frets are laid out so that the guitar sounds "in tune" when played in all keys (called "equal-tempered tuning").

So, after tuning with your electronic tuner you'll need to fine-tune your guitar by ear. Double check your tuning with your electronic tuner, then play some low-position chords to check for accuracy. On a first position G-major chord, for example, you'll probably find the low E-string (fretted at the third fret) sounds a little sharp and needs flattening very slightly.

Many tuning inaccuracies are caused by "relative tuning". This is where you get, for

---

STRING LOADING: GOLDEN RULES
• Some players place the uncut string in the string-post hole and then, by hand, wrap the slack around the post. This is not advised as it may well distort the windings of wound strings.
• Never cut a wound string without first making a right-angled bend. This bend is recommended by most string makers and will prevent the winds (wraps) from distorting or unwinding.
• Never have any overlapping winds around the tuner's string-post. Keep things neat and tidy, and always wind the string in a downward direction under the string-post hole.
• Never leave any slack in the string as it winds around the string-post. This could cause future tuning problems.
• Never leave any excess string hanging from the end of the tuners. Either cut the strings close to the string-post or wind the free length into an interlocking circle.

---

example, your low E-string in tune, and then tune the other strings to that. Tuning across the strings (low to high) from the fifth fret to the open strings (the fourth fret on the G-string to the open B-string) is OK, although any discrepancies that occur with one string will be passed on to the next. You can also use the "harmonic" relative tuning method, where you compare, for example, the harmonics at the fifth and seventh frets. But like any other relative tuning method, this too relies on the accuracy of your ear.

An electronic tuner can take the guess-work out of what is, especially for beginners, an onerous task. However, you do need to learn how to tune by ear too. It's good for your musicianship – and what if you were to forget your electronic tuner on that all-important gig?

Anyway, once you get in tune, check the "sweetness" of your tuning by playing some chords (and if you're going to compare notes on your guitar, use unison or octave intervals). Of course, it will be impossible to get your guitar as in-tune as possible unless you've correctly set your intonation (see p48-49).

Vibrato-equipped guitars are more problematic to tune because in most cases as you sharpen one string the rest go flat. In reality, once the balance between the string tension and the vibrato's spring tension is equalised, you're in tune. But you have to be more patient as far as tuning is concerned with most floating vibrato systems (see Bridge/vibrato: general tips p51).

STRING GAUGES

String "gauge" is the outer diameter of the string, universally measured in inches. Lower numbers (thinner strings) are "lighter" gauge; larger numbers (thicker strings) are "heavier" gauge. The most commonly used set of strings consists of gauges that run (from top E-string to low E-string) from .009" to .042", in other words from nine-thousandths to forty-two-thousandths of an inch. This is usually referred to as a "set of nines". A "set of tens" typically goes from .010" to .046". The thinnest readily-available set are "eights" (.008" to .038"); "elevens" are typically .011" to .049".

Then there are the many "hybrid" sets where, for example, the top three strings of a set of nines are combined with the bottom three strings from the heavier tens. All this makes for a bewildering choice. But remember: if everything else remains the same, the thinner the gauge, the easier the strings will be to fret and bend, but the lighter the tone will be. Conversely, the heavier the gauge, the harder the strings will be to fret, but the bigger the tone will be. So while a set of elevens may well give you the biggest tone, they will be a lot harder to fret and bend compared to nines.

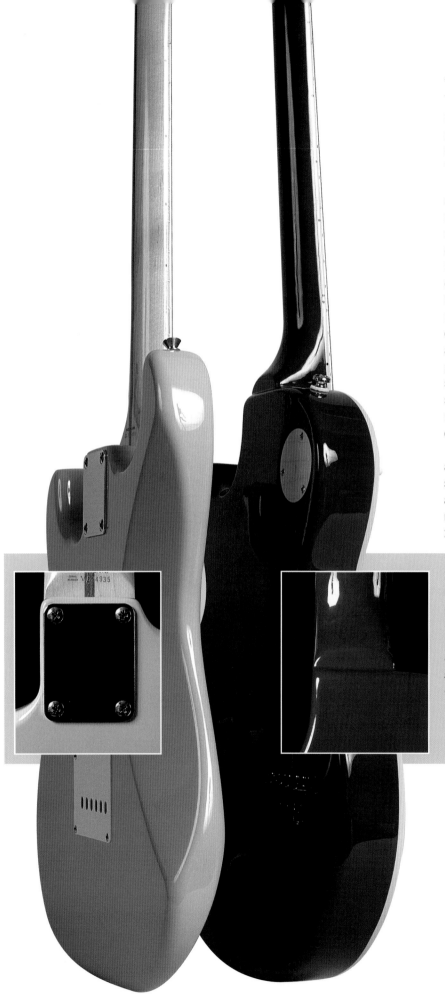

THE JOB OF THE NECK

The neck of an electric guitar is perhaps the most crucial part of the instrument. As well as providing the playing surface – the fingerboard and frets – the main bulk of the neck must feel "right" to the hand.

The physical dimensions of a guitar neck subtly change from brand to brand. There is much debate as to what constitutes the "best" neck, and the dimensions of its width and depth will only tell us part of the story. More important is the shape of the neck. For example, a wider neck won't necessarily feel big in the hand if it's well shaped; a narrower neck can feel bigger if the shaping is less careful. Fender and Gibson, for example, have a huge "catalogue" of neck shapes from their past. Certainly players will rave about a "V" section Fender shape or a '58 Les Paul section. PRS have their wide-fat or "artist" necks; Ibanez, in their virtuoso-rock heyday, created the ultra-thin Wizard profile necks.

Aside from its shape, the neck must be stiff and stable enough to support the considerable string tension. (String makers D'Addario quote a combined tension of 39kg/86lbs with a regular set of .009"-.042" gauge strings on a 25½" scale length, rising to 56kg/123½lbs with

The picture of the two guitars (left) shows the different kinds of neck joint commonly employed by Fender and by Gibson. On the far left is the Fender "bolt-on" neck, joined to the body with four screws through a metal retaining plate. Gibson, however, often use a glued-in neck (near left), which is also referred to as a "set neck" or "fixed neck".

a set of .010"-.052" Lite Top/Heavy Bottom.) Stiff and stable woods are crucial here: hard rock maple (Fender) and mahogany (Gibson) are the classic choices.

The majority of necks are "one-piece". Fender's bolt-on neck is machined from a single slab of maple, for example, while Gibson's Les Paul neck is created from one piece of mahogany with two additional "wings" to create the headstock width. Many modern electrics, with either back-angled or dropped ("pointed") headstocks, use a two-piece design where the headstock is joined onto the main section, which makes the construction more economical. That's not a new idea: the classical guitar uses such a construction both for economy and structural stability.

TYPES OF NECK

"Bolt-on" neck Fender's "bolt-on" neck is a misnomer – but that's what everyone calls it. In fact the neck is simply held to the body with (typically) four *screws*, though some high-end makers do use proper bolts for the job. So long as the neck fits snugly into the neck pocket on the body, there should be minimal movement. The advantage of the bolt-on neck is that it's easy to service or totally replace if necessary.

It is believed that this joint creates a slightly more percussive tone with a quicker attack, or "bite", to the note.

Glued-in neck Gibson's set-neck or glued-in neck is obviously a permanent fixture. You can't easily remove it or alter either the neck pitch or side-to-side alignment. Because the neck and body are joined before finishing – a bolt-on neck can be made and finished totally separate to its body – a set-neck design is often more costly to produce. Tonally, a set-neck design is thought to impart a smoother attack with more perceived sustain. This of course depends on a lot of factors – not least how well the two parts fit together before they are glued.

Fender headstock In side view, Fender's headstock is parallel to the fingerboard face. This makes manufacture more simple than the back-angled Gibson design and more cost-effective in terms of timber. The trouble is that to get enough behind-the-nut string angle (between the tuners and the nut) it's often a necessity to use string-trees – which can snag the strings and cause tuning problems, especially with vibratos.

Gibson headstock The Gibson company has for some time used a back-angled type of headstock that alleviates the need for string trees. However, the acute angle of this back-angled headstock (it is between 14° and 17°) can be a major contributor to the danger of headstock breaks if the guitar is dropped on its back. This weakness is increased by the truss rod adjustment point, situated just behind the nut, which requires a significant amount of wood to be removed at the thinnest and therefore weakest part of the neck.

Fender's straight string-pull You'll often hear people say, "Fender got it right." Starting with the first production electric, Leo Fender designed the headstock so that the strings passed in a straight line over the nut to the tuners. This minimises any sharp angles which, if the nut's string grooves are incorrectly cut, can lead to string-hitching problems – and therefore tuning problems – which are magnified by a non-locking vibrato. Newer designs, like PRS, use a combination of a back-angled headstock (with a less acute angle which aids vibrato return-to-pitch) and straight string pull. Perhaps this is in fact the best of both worlds?

Gibson-style headstock with angled string-pull (left). Fender-style headstock with straight string-pull (right).

Gibson back-angled headstock (near right). Fender headstock parallel to fingerboard face (far right).

SCALE LENGTH

A guitar's quoted scale length refers to the theoretical distance of the vibrating or "speaking" length of the string. In reality the actual scale length is slightly longer to compensate for the fact that to vibrate properly the string must sit above the fingerboard face and the frets. The distance from the top of the frets to the underside of the string is called the string height, and the higher the string height the more the string sharpens in pitch as it's depressed. To compensate for this sharpening effect – which varies from string to string – the theoretical scale length is slightly increased, usually by adjustable bridge saddles. Also, the greater the mass of the string, the more compensation is required.

The scale length, however, remains the fundamental dimension around which all guitars are designed. Apart from determining the nut and bridge positions, the scale length is the crucial dimension from which the fret positions are calculated. For example, the 12th fret position is exactly half of the quoted theoretical scale length.

Fender's primary scale length is 648mm (25½"). Gibson say their scale is 628mm (24¾"), although it actually measures closer to 24.6" than 24.75". PRS have popularised the "in between" scale of 635mm (25"). The scale length – along with the distance and angle of the string behind the nut to the tuners, and the

The Fender-style nut (top) sits in a channel, while the Gibson-style nut (above) sits at the end of the fingerboard, a point worth bearing in mind when it comes to nut replacement.

distance of string behind the bridge saddles to the string anchor point or tailpiece – affects the tension and perceived feel of the strings when you're fretting and bending. In theory, with all factors identical and the same string gauge, a 648mm (25½") scale length will have a tighter feel, and a 628mm (24¾") scale will have a slightly slacker feel.

Tonally, too, the scale length plays a part. Many designers and players feel a longer scale

emphasises string definition. Obviously, the smaller the scale length a guitar has, the closer together the frets will be – which may make a guitar with such a scale less desirable if you play primarily in the upper fret areas yet like big and wide frets.

TOP NUT

The nut (or "top nut") serves the important purpose of providing the start of the string's speaking length. It's the opposite point to the bridge or bridge saddle. It will also determine both the string height at (primarily) the first fret and the overall string spacing in the lower fret positions. A badly cut nut, where the string grooves impede the path of the string itself, will also contribute to tuning problems. All in all, the nut is an important feature.

Historically, top nuts were made from ivory or bone, but today most will be made from some kind of synthetic material, apart from in the really high end of the market. Of course, different materials will mostly affect the open-string tone of the guitar. A new breed of friction-reducing nuts, like Graph Tech's Trem Nut, use a graphite/plastic mix to help minimise string-groove friction. This is an important consideration for guitars with non-locking vibratos. Intriguingly, a soft nut material can often affect both tuning and tonal efficiency; upgrading to a superior material can dramatically improve your guitar.

The three photographs here show some of the ways in which compensation is provided for the sharpening effect of the strings as they are depressed towards the frets. Gibson's early wrapover bridge (above, on a Les Paul Junior) relied on an angled ridge to increase the theoretical scale length.

The PRS bridge (above) took the idea of the Gibson wrapover bridge and improved it by using a pre-compensated ridge tailored for different string gauges.

Fender's original six-saddle Stratocaster bridge (reissued version, above) allows the player relatively easily to adjust individual string compensation. Shown above is the vibrato version of the Strat bridge; there are non-vibrato versions too, sometimes nicknamed "hardtail" bridges.

JAG-STANG SCALE LENGTH 24 INCHES

LES PAUL SCALE LENGTH 24¾ INCHES

PRS SCALE LENGTH 25 INCHES

STRAT SCALE LENGTH 25½ INCHES

Fret positions are calculated from scale length. The 12th fret, for example, is half the quoted theoretical scale length.

Four different scale lengths are displayed here: the Fender Jag-Stang (far left) has one of the shortest at 24"; the Gibson Les Paul (second left) has a scale length quoted at 24¾"; PRS (left) opt for a scale midway between Gibson and Fender, at 25"; Fender's 25½" scale (as on this Strat, right) is the longest standard scale length on an electric.

Shown here are two versions of the popular box-section truss-rod used by many makers. The rod sits in a U-shape aluminium extrusion.

This example (left) of the box-section truss-rod has the adjustment at the neck end; the example at the top of the page has the adjustment at the body end.

WHAT IS A TRUSS-ROD?

Inside virtually all electric guitars sold today you'll find an adjustable truss-rod. It runs down the centre of the neck. Non-adjustable truss-rods were installed on early steel-string acoustic guitars for added neck stiffness. But the main job of an adjustable truss-rod is to provide adjustment of the neck's "relief", and not stiffness.

The most simple truss-rod dates back to the original design patented in 1923 by Gibson. (The original patent shows a convex rod. This was changed by Gibson in 1950 to the modern and more effective curving concave design.) A metal rod is installed in a curved channel in the centre of the neck. At one end (usually the body end) it's fixed in place; at the other end, typically at the nut, the rod is threaded and fitted with an adjusting nut and collar. Despite a number of variations on this basic design, the net result remains the same: when the adjusting nut is tightened, the neck moves to correct a concave bow. (A concave-bow neck dips slightly in the middle; a convex-bow neck curves slightly upwards in the middle.) If the truss-rod already has tension on it and, for example, has a convex bow, slackening the nut will help "straighten" the neck.

Recently many companies have switched to a dual-action rod. It's basically the same idea but, thanks to a clever nut and/or reverse thread arrangement, when the nut is slackened it creates pressure on the neck to create a concave bow. This can be an advantage with bigger, very stable necks used with light-gauge strings where the normal single-action rod – even fully slackened – does not provide enough relief (see Checking Relief following this).

Many (mainly Far Eastern) guitars use a box-section adjustable truss. British guitar maker Chris Eccleshall is credited with this design. The rod lies within a U-shaped aluminium extrusion which is placed in a flat channel, with its open side face down, directly below the fingerboard. As the rod is tightened it compresses the aluminium extrusion which in turn applies upward pressure on the fingerboard to correct the bow.

When you buy a new guitar you'll usually find included an owner's manual and a truss-rod adjustment key, and the manual will provide some basic info on making any necessary adjustments yourself. Conversely, most repairers generally discourage their customers from attempting any truss-rod adjustment. This is usually good advice, but the conflicting signals from manufacturer and repairer can leave the beginner confused. So what's the mystery?

Paradoxically, truss-rod adjustment can be both simple and complex at the same time. On the simple side, a minor adjustment either to straighten a neck with too much concave bow (achieved by tightening the rod) or to relieve a convex bow (by slackening the rod) is possibly all that's needed to make some dramatic improvements, and can easily save you a trip to your repairman.

On the complex side, there are two main considerations: (a) the majority of truss-rods have a delayed rather than immediate effect, because it takes time for the neck to "settle" after adjustment; and (b) adjusting the rod will simultaneously alter other aspects of the set-up such as overall string height, the string height at the nut, intonation and so on. Furthermore, the actual effect any rod adjustment has on the neck will vary between instruments according to the type of rod and the different woods used for the neck's construction. Even on two identical models, the rods can have differing effects. Sometimes, even with new guitars, slackening the rod fully still won't have the desired effect, and other measures become necessary. But with new instruments, that's what the warranty is for. Also, don't forget that necks are subject to movement caused by changes of temperature and humidity, so be prepared to tweak the rod when necessary.

CHECKING RELIEF

There is a myth that a well set-up guitar will not buzz. When you think about it, this is impossible. The simple contact of vibrating metal strings on the metal frets will easily buzz

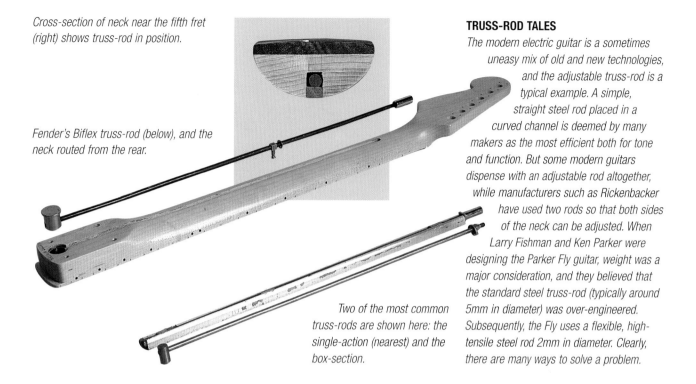

Cross-section of neck near the fifth fret (right) shows truss-rod in position.

Fender's Biflex truss-rod (below), and the neck routed from the rear.

Two of the most common truss-rods are shown here: the single-action (nearest) and the box-section.

TRUSS-ROD TALES

The modern electric guitar is a sometimes uneasy mix of old and new technologies, and the adjustable truss-rod is a typical example. A simple, straight steel rod placed in a curved channel is deemed by many makers as the most efficient both for tone and function. But some modern guitars dispense with an adjustable rod altogether, while manufacturers such as Rickenbacker have used two rods so that both sides of the neck can be adjusted. When Larry Fishman and Ken Parker were designing the Parker Fly guitar, weight was a major consideration, and they believed that the standard steel truss-rod (typically around 5mm in diameter) was over-engineered. Subsequently, the Fly uses a flexible, high-tensile steel rod 2mm in diameter. Clearly, there are many ways to solve a problem.

if you pick hard enough. We can conclude that buzz is part of the sound produced from an electric guitar. What we're trying to do is to minimise buzz in favour of the pure note.

To minimise buzz caused by the strings hitting the frets, a slight amount of concave bow to the neck (dipping in the middle) is usually necessary due to the vibrating strings' elliptical shape. The small amount of "gap" in the neck (concave bow) is called relief and is usually (not always) necessary for a buzz-free action. This concave bow really occurs between the first fret and roughly where the heel of the neck starts (typically somewhere between the 14th and 16th fret). Relief is measured at the mid-point: the seventh-to-eighth fret.

With your guitar in playing position, fret the low E-string at the first fret with your left hand and the 14th fret with your right hand. Now look at the seventh or eighth fret. There should be a small gap between this fret and the string. That's the relief. The shots here should help you recognise generous relief **A**, average relief **B**, and virtually no relief **C**.

The amount of necessary relief varies according to string gauge, string height and how hard you play. For example, if you use light-gauge strings with a low string height and a light touch you'll probably need less relief and a virtually straight neck. However, before you make any adjustments you need to measure the relief and evaluate the neck's condition.

MEASURING NECK RELIEF

• Just playing your guitar (normally, through a clean, not distorted, amp) can give you a good indication of how much relief you need. If, for example, you're getting fret buzz on most strings when you play on the lower frets it could mean you don't have enough relief. If the lower frets sound fine, but as you move up the neck you're getting more buzz, it may mean you've got too much relief. Note, however, that this latter scenario could also mean there's a more serious problem that the truss-rod can't cure. Part of any guitar neck is held firmly in

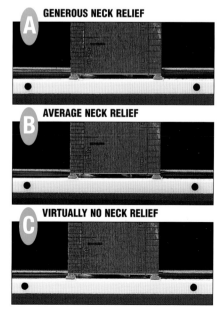

A GENEROUS NECK RELIEF

B AVERAGE NECK RELIEF

C VIRTUALLY NO NECK RELIEF

the body. The main, unsupported length is pulled slightly forwards by the string tension; the resulting concave bow can be corrected by the truss-rod. However, if there's a fault in the neck itself (maybe the truss-rod is too short, or the timber too weak) the neck can bend at this fulcrum point creating an "up-tilt" which can't be corrected by the truss-rod.

If you don't realise this and continue to tighten the rod, you may create an S-shape bend where the main playing area has a convex bow (because you've over-tightned the truss-rod) and the final part of the neck still tilts up because the neck itself is at fault.

• Place a capo at the first fret. Press the G string down at the 14th fret. Look out for a small gap of approximately 0.25mm (.010") between the top of the seventh-to-ninth fret and the underside of the string. You can measure this gap with feeler gauges **D** or a steel ruler (or even use a light-gauge plectrum, approximately 0.5mm thick, as a rough guide).

• Move the capo in place at either the seventh or eighth fret, and with your right hand fret the last fret. Now measure the gap over the 14th fret (as described above). If this second gap is a lot more than the first relief measurement, it could mean that your neck has a fault. In this case do not attempt to tighten the rod; take your guitar to a pro.

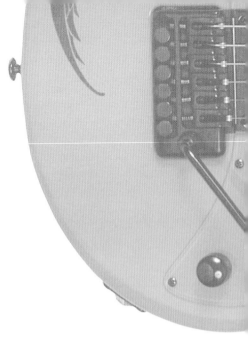

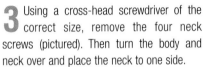

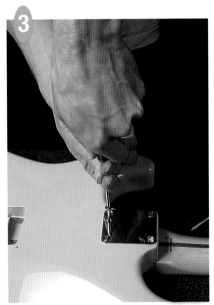

3 Using a cross-head screwdriver of the correct size, remove the four neck screws (pictured). Then turn the body and neck over and place the neck to one side.

4 Cut a shim with scissors (pictured) to the appropriate size.

5 Place the shim between the end of the neck pocket and the two screws furthest into the body (pictured). A couple of small dots of PVA glue will hold the shim in place, or you can use double-sided adhesive tape. Then re-assemble the guitar. Put some tension back on the strings and reset the saddles. If everything seems OK, carefully reset the string height as described on p44. If, however, the shim turns out to be too low or too high, don't worry. Just remove the neck, take out the shim and try again.

MORE BOLT-ON NECK ADJUSTMENTS

Unless a bolt-on neck is really well fitted, the chances are it may move sideways if it's roughly handled or knocked. It's usually pretty subtle, but the first check you want to make is to see if your neck moves.

Hold the guitar in a seated playing position and firmly but not roughly push down on the neck **Ⓐ**. Did you feel it move? Did it creak? Don't worry if it did move. Pull in the opposite direction and it should move back again. What you've established is the likelihood that your guitar neck will move in the future, and that's not ideal. But the cure can be simple.

First, measure the distance from the outer strings, at the 12th fret, to the edge of the fingerboard **Ⓑ**. The distance should be the

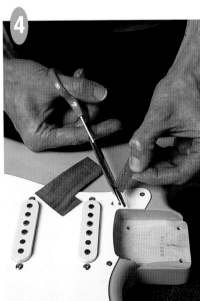

The angle of a guitar's neck relative to its body face is called the neck "pitch". The side views of the guitars here (right) show the relatively shallow pitch of a typical bolt-on-neck Strat-style guitar (far right), which is contrasted by the steeper pitch of a set-neck Les Paul-style guitar (near right).

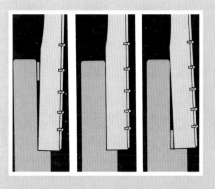

Three exaggerated drawings of a bolt-on neck guitar (above). With a shim added as far into the neck pocket as possible (right) the neck pitch is increased. Without a shim (centre) the fingerboard is virtually parallel to the face of the body; this may limit action adjustment. In extreme cases a shim placed at the tip of the neck pocket (left) creates an upward tilt of the neck, although in reality this is rarely required.

ADJUSTING A BOLT-ON NECK

In theory the face of a bolt-on neck will be parallel to the face of the guitar's body. In practice the neck often tilts back slightly, and this back angle is called the neck "pitch". The main reason for the pitch is so that the correct string height can be set. The Les Paul design has a carved-top body, so the neck leaves the body at quite a steep angle, and many players find this more comfortable.

It's quite important to understand the relationship between the bridge height and the neck pitch. On a bolt-on-neck Stratocaster, for example, the individually adjustable saddles – especially the pressed-steel type of a vintage vibrato bridge – have a limited range of height adjustment. You may find that even with the saddles as low as they can go the action is still too high. By slightly increasing the neck pitch the action can be made lower. (Viewed from the bass side of the guitar, the tip of the neck heel acts as the fulcrum point. Think of a see-saw. To the left of that point the neck drops; to the right it rises.) Imagine the reverse situation: that even with the saddles adjusted to their full height, the action is too low, so you need to reduce the neck pitch – possibly even creating an upward tilt. The saddles-at-lowest/action-too-high scenario is the most common, whereas the saddles-at-highest/action-too-low scenario, where you need to reduce the neck pitch, is actually quite rare.

Fender's American Standard series guitars have a four-screw neck-to-body fixing plus a micro-tilt adjustment which makes neck-pitch adjustment easy. For bolt-on-neck guitars without this micro-tilt adjustment – and that's the majority – you'll need to add a neck shim to increase neck pitch. A shim is a small piece of thin, hard material – ideally wood veneer, hard plastic sheet or hard cardboard. Cigarette packets or similar will work in an emergency, but harder materials are preferable. Here's what you do.

STRAT-STYLE NECK-PITCH ADJUSTMENT

1 If the guitar is fitted with a vibrato, place a stack of business cards or the vibrato backplate (pictured) under the back of the vibrato bridge.

2 Slacken strings, place a capo at the first fret (pictured). Then remove the vibrato system's arm if there is one. Lay the guitar on a flat surface, face down.

MEASURING RELIEF WITH FEELER GAUGE

ADJUSTING GIBSON-STYLE TRUSS-ROD (COVER OFF)

NECK SLIPPED UP TO ADJUST FENDER VINTAGE-STYLE TRUSS-ROD

ADJUSTING THE TRUSS ROD

Once you've followed the steps to evaluate the relief you can adjust the truss-rod if necessary. Always follow the maker's recommendations and use the supplied truss-rod key or Allen wrench. Before you touch the truss-rod read *If In Doubt... Don't* below.

For guitars with nut-end adjustment **E** the basic procedure is as follows.

• If you need less relief, tighten the truss-rod adjusting nut by turning it clockwise. Obviously you may need you to remove the coverplate behind the nut. If you have too little relief, slacken the adjusting nut by turning it anti-clockwise (counter-clockwise).

Vintage Fender-style guitars have the rod adjustment at the body end, which creates a little more work.

• Having evaluated the relief, slacken the strings and place a capo at the first fret.

• Turn the guitar over. Undo (but don't fully remove) the neck screws. Slip the neck upwards **F** to see the cross-head adjusting nut.

• Make your adjustment, re-tighten the neck screws, remove the capo and tune up. Check the relief again and if you need to make further adjustments repeat the above steps.

Note that when tightening the truss-rod it is advisable to slacken the string tension slightly. Because metal strings are in contact with metal frets you must always expect a certain degree of fret buzz, magnified by how hard you hit the string. Always listen for fret buzz through an amp.

IF IN DOUBT... DON'T

It's not surprising that even many pro players won't attempt rod adjustments themselves, but if you feel inclined to try any small adjustments in accordance with the manufacturers' manual, here are some tips.

• Always use the correct tool for the job.

• Never force the adjuster if it feels very tight.

• Make any adjustments in very small degrees at a time and monitor progress. Usually the correct adjustment is achieved within about a quarter turn in the appropriate direction. Avoid making adjustments greater than this.

• Leave some time for the neck to settle between adjustments.

• If you have any doubts, take the guitar back to the shop or a qualified repairer.

The techniques described on these pages apply to virtually all bolt-on-neck guitars, including modern examples such as the Music Man Silhouette illustrated here.

same on either side. However, a greater distance on the treble side can be useful: it will make hammer-on and pull-off techniques easier, becasue it is less likely that you'll slip off the board.

Manhandle the neck until you achieve the right position. Lay the guitar face down on your work surface and tighten (but don't over-tighten) the neck screws. Sometimes this is all you need to do to cure any movement. Now, see if you can move the neck under reasonable pressure. If you can't, you're OK: most bolt-ons just need a little tightening from time to time.

If the neck still moves, remove it (as described opposite) and check the condition of the neck pocket and the bottom of the neck. Are there any loose wood shavings? Are the surfaces rough? The flatter the surfaces, the more neck-to-body contact and the more stable the joint will be. Don't try to smooth the neck pocket – take it to a pro. But one thing that you can do that might help is to apply some dry lubricant such as candle wax to the neck screws  and then re-assemble the guitar. This simple tip may allow slightly more pressure to be applied without damaging the screw heads, and thus cure any movement.

Removing a bolt-on neck may seem dramatic on your first attempt but so long as you use the correct tools, lubricate the screws and don't over-tighten them you'll be OK. *Never* force a screw. If it doesn't want to move then leave it and seek pro advice. Conversely, if your neck still moves following the basic advice given here, consult a pro.

A CHECKING FOR NECK MOVEMENT

B MEASURING OUTER STRING DISTANCES

C LUBRICATING NECK SCREWS

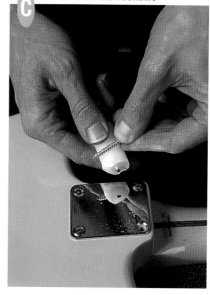

TYPES OF TUNERS

On most modern electric guitars, except some of the cheapest, you should find a pretty decent set of tuners (machine heads). Most are pre-lubricated, fully-enclosed tuners based on the original Grover/Schaller design. These have a high gear ratio, which means you have to turn the button more to get one rotation of the string post, giving a fine degree of adjustment. They also have a small tension-adjustment screw at the end of the button.

On some electrics you'll find tuners modelled on the older Kluson design. Japanese reissue Fenders, for example, use this type with a "split" string-post and non-adjustable metal buttons. Certain Epiphones use a similar tuner but with a vintage-like green-tinged plastic "tulip" button or a keystone-shaped button, and a standard string-post. Despite their vintage look, most have a higher gear ratio than the originals.

A new breed of locking tuners began to appear in the 1980s which lock the string onto the string-post. Specifically designed for guitars with non-locking vibratos, they bring an end to all that fiddly winding of the string-end around the string-post. Installing strings is very

Adjusting the screw on the end of a tuner button (above) in order to create a firmer and more even feel to its operation.

easy and you can be confident that any potential movement that can cause string slippage and therefore return-to-pitch problems will be eliminated. But locking tuners are a fine upgrade for any guitar, with or without vibrato, as they make re-stringing very quick and should aid overall tuning stability. The US-made Sperzel heads lead the way,

though locking tuners are also available from makers such as Schaller (as used by Fender), Gotoh, Grover and LSR.

TUNER ADJUSTMENT

There is little alteration necessary with most modern tension-adjustable tuners. When you change strings, you should check that the fixing nut on the face of the headstock is tight. If it's loose you'll need to tighten it with a box spanner of the correct size. *Never* use pliers.

The small screw at the end of the tuner button affects the feel of the machine head. Technically it doesn't reduce what is called "backlash", the free play of the tuner between clockwise and anti/counter-clockwise rotation. Tightening the screw (pictured left) will create a firmer feel. Don't over-tighten or tighten it so far that you can't easily move the button. Your aim here is to get an even feel (tight or slack, whatever you like) on all the tuners.

PRS use their own design of Schaller-made locking tuners which are without the white nylon washer between the button and the housing, leaving just the bent metal washer in place. PRS tighten their tuners for quite a positive (some would say stiff) action, based on

Shown here (right and below) is a variety of different tuner types, ranging from simple non-adjustable versions to more sophisticated adjustable and locking models. A number of manufacturers and brands are involved; this is just a selection of those available.

Schaller: fully enclosed, tension-adjustable.

Gotoh Magnum Lock: tension-adjustable, locking.

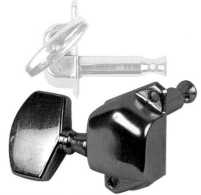

Economy type: non-adjustable.

Kluson vintage-style: non-adjustable.

Sperzel Trim-Lok: tension-adjustable, locking.

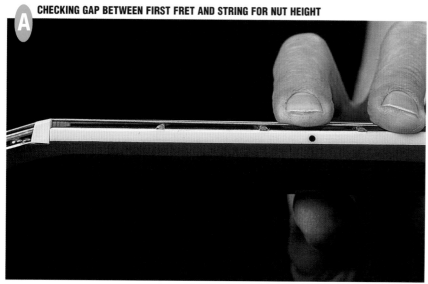

CHECKING GAP BETWEEN FIRST FRET AND STRING FOR NUT HEIGHT

LUBRICATING NUT GROOVE WITH PENCIL

HEIGHT-ADJUSTABLE BRASS NUT

their belief that the firmer the tuner the more stable the tuning.

Finally, it's worth underlining that tuning problems caused by the nut or by the string tree, or simply by bad string attachment, will not be cured by the tuner, whatever its type.

CHECKING NUT HEIGHT

Our main concern with the top nut is to ensure that it is cut to the "correct" height and has friction-free string slots. Altering or replacing a nut is definitely a pro's job, and nut replacement is usually necessary when you have your guitar re-fretted.

Most new production guitars have nuts that are cut a little too high. This may make it harder to press the strings down and fret them (and might cause intonation problems), but it is simpler for a repairer to lower your nut height than to increase it.

To check your top nut height, first fret each string between the second and third frets **A**. Ideally there should be a very small gap above the first fret and the bottom of each string. Even if it is almost touching, don't worry – the open, unfretted string may still vibrate cleanly. If the open string buzzes, then it probably means that the nut slot is too low – but check both your neck relief (see p29) and string action height (see p44/45).

To check if the string groove in the nut is impeding the return-to-pitch of the string, pick an open string and bend it by pushing down on the string *behind* the nut. Can you hear any clicks? This will indicate a tight string groove in the nut. Does the string come back into tune? Re-tune and try again. So long as your strings are properly stretched, a behind-the-nut up-bend of around a semitone should come back in tune. Again, getting the string grooves perfectly smooth is a tricky job. If you've got problems, lift the string out of the groove, rub a soft pencil lead (graphite) **B** into the groove and return the string. Try those bends again. The graphite lubrication may have helped but won't necessarily cure the problem.

The ever-resourceful British maker Gordon-Smith uses a height-adjustable brass nut **C**. It's a neat idea. If over a long period the nut slots become worn you can loosen the nut with the two screws, place a thin shim under the nut to raise it, and if necessary re-cut the slots. Of course, if you just want to raise your string height, for slide or bottleneck playing, it's very easy – just use a thicker shim.

PRO'S PERSPECTIVE: NEW NUTS FOR OLD

Hugh Manson, a UK repairman and custom-builder for the likes of John Paul Jones, says the main reason to replace a top nut is because it's too low, either from the abrasive action of the strings, or when a re-fret sets the new frets higher than the old ones. Another problem occurs when players increase the gauge of strings they use. "Never try to force a heavier-gauge string into an old nut slot that was cut for a lighter gauge," advises Manson. "At worst you may crack the nut, or suffer from tuning problems as the new string sticks in the old slot." A repairman will use special tools to cut and/or widen the slots. When it

comes to nut replacement, some guitars are problematic. "The ones I hate are those 1970s Fenders where the thick polyester finish is sprayed over the nut. Getting the old nut out is difficult." The same can apply to many Gibson guitars where the nut sits at the end of the fingerboard but is partially recessed into the neck wood and then sprayed over. Many modern guitars, including those of PRS for example, have the nut fixed after finishing, so nut replacement is relatively easy. "A nut has a finite life," concludes Manson. "It must be solidly fixed, but removable in the future when replacement becomes necessary."

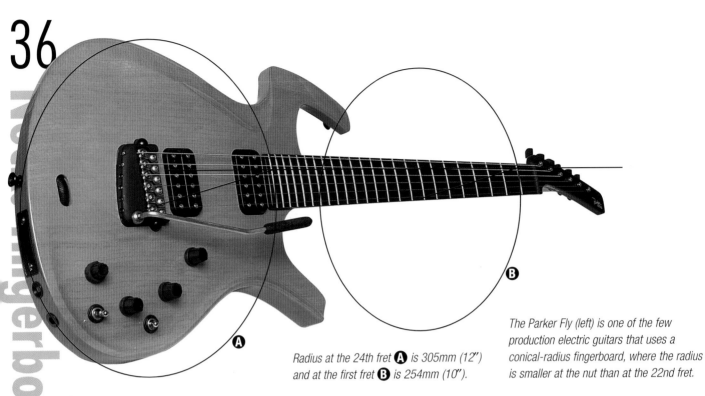

Radius at the 24th fret **A** is 305mm (12″) and at the first fret **B** is 254mm (10″).

The Parker Fly (left) is one of the few production electric guitars that uses a conical-radius fingerboard, where the radius is smaller at the nut than at the 22nd fret.

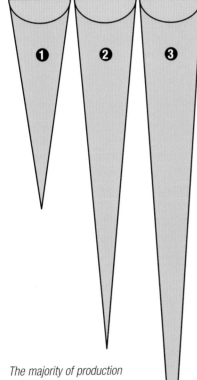

The majority of production electrics use a fingerboard radius that is constant. Original Fenders (and reissues) use a small 184mm radius ❶, Gibson use a flatter 305mm ❷, and many Floyd Rose-equipped guitars use an even flatter 406mm ❸.

ABOUT FINGERBOARDS

The fingerboard holds the frets and provides the playing surface of the instrument. Obvious, really. But, as ever, the role of the fingerboard is more complex. Made from a hard-wearing hardwood – typically rosewood or ebony – the fingerboard is usually unfinished. Only if a light-coloured wood such as maple is used is a finish applied, to protect it from getting dirty.

Some makers such as Music Man use a light oil finish on both the maple neck and fingerboard, and this does get dirty. Some players like it; others (including shop owners) often don't. Back in the 1970s Fender used a very thick finish on their maple fingerboards, and this may be why people think that maple and rosewood 'boards feel different.

In reality, with the modern choice of typically higher-gauge fretwire, the fingerboard material makes little difference to its playing feel. Tonally, however, the fingerboard will have an effect. Maple is perceived to have a bright and twangy tone, contrasted by the warmer tone of the softer rosewood. Ebony is the hardest and smoothest wood used for the job, and creates a bright sound with a lot of definition. But as ever the "sound" of wood is a highly subjective area.

PRO'S PERSPECTIVE: FRETFULNESS

Fret wear, unless extreme, rarely requires a total re-fret; usually the repairer can level the frets, then re-shape ("crown" or "dress") them to a smooth, dome-like section. Experienced repairer Tim Shaw, a manager at Guild's Custom Shop, says: "Every time the frets are re-crowned, the flatter they get. In extreme cases they become so flat that your intonation goes, and your only option is a re-fret.

"One of the main reasons for a re-fret is when a twisted neck can't be straightened by the rod, or if the radius needs to be increased. Some players will prefer a re-fret instead of levelling, if they like a high fretwire. Others may simply fancy a change.

"The hardest and therefore most expensive fret jobs are those involving guitars with bound fingerboards." Finished maple fingerboards – Rickenbackers, old 1970s Fenders – are problematic too, but an unbound, unfinished rosewood 'board is probably the most straightforward, says Shaw. "A repairer who can't re-fret a stiff-necked old Les Paul Junior is really in trouble," he laughs.

FINGERBOARD RADIUS

Much more important to the player is the slight radius (camber, or curving) of the fingerboard. Combined with the size of the frets and the overall set-up, this is what contributes most to different fingerboard feels.

Radius is measured by considering the fingerboard as a wedge from a cylinder of a certain radius. Fender originally used a small 184mm (7¼") radius, although US/Mexican-made Fenders now uniformly use a flatter 241mm/9½" radius. Gibson went for a flatter 305mm (12") radius, PRS use an "in between" 254mm (10"), and Parker use a compound "conical" radius increasing from nut to top fret, from approximately 254mm (10") to 305mm (12"), so that the board is flatter in its upper reaches. Modern rock guitars typically use a flatter radius from 356mm (14") upwards.

So why all the options? Fender's vintage radius feels great for comfortable chording, but with a low action, high-fret bends can lead to "choking" (the bent string colliding against a higher fret). The only way to stop this is to raise the action or flatten the fingerboard radius, hence Fender's current 241mm (9½") radius.

But fashions constantly change. Currently we're seeing 241mm (9½") to 305mm (12") radiuses – which suit virtually any playing style – fitted with high but not too wide frets, and neck shapes that are chunkier in cross-section. This is a distinct contrast to the 80s/early-90s virtuoso "speed-is-everything" designs which use a much flatter fingerboard with heavy-gauge frets and a thin-depth neck. At first such thin necks seem very comfortable, but many players find them tiring for extended sessions. But the "conical" (or compound) radius makes a lot of sense as it provides comfort in the lower positions and very easy high-fret bendability. In reality, unless your guitar uses very small-gauge fretwire, the frets rather than the fingerboard provide the real playing surface. Made from nickel silver, the fret is pushed and sometimes glued into sawn fret-slots on the fingerboard. Once seated, the frets are levelled and polished to provide a smooth, buzz-free playing surface. Originally both Fender and Gibson used very narrow and quite low frets.

Wider frets became popular for a smoother feel, but as string gauges came down and string-bending became much more popular, makers and players realised that higher frets made strings easier to bend. Wide and low frets were popular for their smooth feel, but if the top of the fret (the "crown") is too flat you can get intonation problems. Likewise if the fret is very high you have to be careful how you fret as it's easy to sharpen notes when you play with uneven finger pressure, especially within a tricky chord.

CHECKING FOR FRET BUZZ

Fret buzz can be caused by too-low string height (see p43), too much or too little neck relief (see p29), or isolated individual height problems (where, for example, one fret has popped out of its fingerboard slot). Always test for fret buzz through your amp. Bear in mind that minor buzzing due to hard playing and the proximity of metal-to-metal (string against fret) is unavoidable. Nonetheless, play every string at every fret and if you hear a deadening clonk at, for example, the 12th fret, it could mean either that this fret is too low or that the next fret (the 13th in this example) is too high. Note the problems, and have a pro check your guitar.

TYPES OF FRETWIRE

Here we show a selection of fretwire of varying sizes, illustrated on actual fingerboards as well as in cross-section. Fender's "vintage" fretwire (near right) is of a relatively small gauge. A fretwire of larger section is fitted by Gibson (centre), while the Jackson fingerboard pictured (far right) sports wire of a larger size, usually called "jumbo" fretwire. The illustrations below each example represent a cross-section view of the individual type of fretwire.

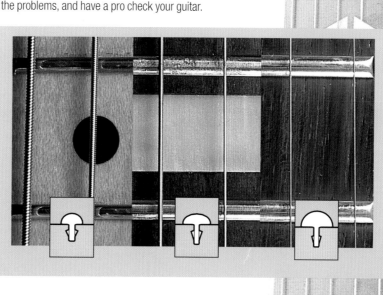

An original Gibson Tune-o-matic bridge and stud tailpiece is pictured here (above). Compare the bridge section to that of the modern-style Tune-o-matic (below, right) and the lack of slot-head height adjusters is evident on the old-style type; the height here has to be set using the thumb-wheels at each end. Gibson first used the Tune-o-matic bridge on their Les Paul Custom model of 1954, and applied it to the Les Paul Gold Top (as pictured left) in the following year. Since then a variety of Tune-o-matic-style bridges have been used on many other guitars.

This Gibson Les Paul Gold Top features a stud tailpiece and Tune-o-matic bridge, a design that has influenced many other hardware makers since its introduction by Gibson during the mid 1950s.

WHY A BRIDGE?

The bridge plays a major role on any electric or acoustic stringed instrument – fretted or un-fretted. If the top nut and then the subsequent frets provide the start point of an individual note's string length, the bridge (specifically its saddles) is the end point. But unlike the top nut, which is only "in play" on open strings, the bridge is always in the game – from open strings to the highest fretted note. On all electric guitars the bridge is also the point at which most intonation adjustments are carried out so that a guitar will play as in-tune as possible. Of course, your bridge can't solve intonation problems caused by the top nut, the frets or the condition of your strings.

The bridge plays the fundamental role of transmitting the strings' vibrations to the body, too. The material of the electric guitar will absorb and reflect this energy in varying ways and thereby produce the instrument's tone and sustain characteristics. These are then hugely magnified and coloured further by the pickups, electrics and, of course, the amplifier. It therefore follows that the material of the bridge and its construction are crucial to the creation

Tune-o-matic modern style

Leo Quan Badass

of your eventual tone. The bridges on early solidbody electric guitars like the Telecaster now seem crude and simplistic. But many believe this simplicity is tonally beneficial, providing the most direct link between string and body. Perhaps that's why designers and manufacturers still use seemingly archaic bridge designs, such as Gibson's one-piece "wrapover" bridge/tailpiece and the three-saddle Telecaster bridge.

TYPES OF FIXED BRIDGE

The simplest form of electric guitar bridge is the fixed type, without any of a vibrato's facility to change the pitch of the strings. For the player, a fixed-bridge instrument is usually quicker to tune and easier to maintain than a vibrato-equipped guitar – a point often overlooked by beginners.

Telecaster Crude but highly effective, the original Telecaster bridge uses three saddles, with the strings anchored in recessed cups on the back of the guitar. Each saddle is adjustable for height and intonation, but with three saddles the adjustment is obviously only available for *pairs* of strings. Six-saddle Tele

bridges are now commonplace, yet many players prefer the tonal qualities associated with three-saddle types.

One-piece "wrapover" The very earliest Gibson Les Pauls used an inefficient "trapeze" tailpiece and bridge-bar assembly. As the strings passed *under* the bridge bar, any kind of right-hand palm muting was impossible. This was quickly changed to a one-piece wrapover or stud bridge/tailpiece (during 1953). The strings anchor in holes at the front of the bridge then wrap over the curved top of the unit. There is no individual string intonation adjustment, but two grub screws locate onto the height-adjustable mounting studs to provide overall intonation adjustment. This simple design is still used today and forms the basis for the PRS Stop-Tail, Leo Quan's Badass and Wilkinson's GB-100, all of which are combination bridge/tailpiece types.

Tune-o-matic In 1954 Gibson switched to their third "electric" design, creating the classic Tune-o-matic bridge and separate stud tailpiece. The Tune-o-matic has individual string-intonation adjustment but only overall

height adjustment. The old-style designs use two thumb-wheels for height adjustment, but many modern guitars now use a Tune-o-matic design that is fitted with an easier-to-use slot-head height adjustment.

Leo Quan Badass Another popular bridge design which appeared in the 1970s, this combines the tonally efficient one-piece wrapover bridge/tailpiece with a Tune-o-matic's individually-adjustable saddles. Schaller, the German hardware manufacturer, make a similar but more bulky version.

PRS Stop-Tail Although PRS were originally known for their highly efficient vibrato, their fixed-bridge Stop-Tail bridge is a finely designed and engineered version of the one-piece wrapover concept. It uses studs of a larger diameter to stop the bridge tilting forward, and a pre-compensated ridge that provides near perfect intonation with .009" and .010" gauge strings. PRS also make a version – much like the Badass – with separate saddles that supply individual string intonation for players needing more precise intonation and/or using heavier gauge strings.

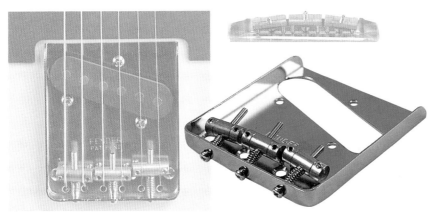

Telecaster three-saddle (showing strings fed through from back, left)

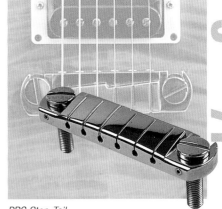

PRS Stop-Tail

Telecaster six-saddle

One-piece wrapover

Wilkinson GB-100

HISTORY OF THE VIBRATO

A guitar's vibrato adds more complexity to the instrument, both for the manufacturer and the player. But from the pioneering days of the electric guitar the ability to manipulate pitch – originally to simulate lap steel-type effects and violin-like vibrato – has been an important goal. Back in 1929 Clayton Orr "Doc" Kauffman patented a sideways-moving vibrato called the Vibrola which was offered as an option on Rickenbacker's 1935 Bakelite lap-steel-size Electro Spanish guitar, their first "conventional" guitar. In the early 1940s another electric guitar pioneer, Les Paul, put together his famous "Log" with a vibrato device that looks crude, home-made... and very similar to Kauffman's Vibrola. Later in that decade Paul Bigsby started work on his vibrato at the request of Merle Travis whose Gibson L-10 had a Kauffman Vibrola that wouldn't stay in tune. The eventual Bigsby became standard on Gretsch and Gibson guitars from the early 1950s – and in the late 1990s they're enjoying quite a revival. However, few would disagree that the "modern" vibrato did not surface until 1954. The Fender Stratocaster's Synchronised Tremolo, as it was called, differed considerably from prior designs, having an all-in-one combined bridge and tailpiece. Leo Fender subsequently toyed with numerous other vibrato designs like the '58 Fender Jazzmaster vibrato with a lock intended to stabilise the unit should you break a string, but the Strat type remains in wide use. There were many innovative vibrato designs introduced during the 1960s, not least the Burns Marvin which featured a Strat-influenced vibrato with a knife-edge pivot system to maximise the vibrato's return-to-pitch accuracy. But it wasn't until the late 1970s that the next major commercially-important vibrato surfaced. In 1979 Floyd Rose was granted a patent for his double-locking vibrato. Based on the Fender Strat design, it added locks at saddle and nut, and offered very wide pitch travel: it could be down-bent (or "dive-bombed") until the strings went slack *and* came back in-tune.

The addition of a set of fine-tuners was patented in 1985 and, in no small part due to the influence of Eddie Van Halen, the double-locking fine-tuned vibrato design became synonymous with the modern, virtuoso-led electric guitar. There were other high-performance designs from makers such as Kahler and Steinberger, but without the lasting impact of the Floyd Rose.

Not everyone wanted the hassle of the double-locking system. Leo Fender reworked his classic system for G&L's S-500 in 1982, and two years later Paul Reed Smith patented his vibrato design that updated Fender's original by using a six-screw knife-edge pivot with locking tuners and a friction-reducing nut. By 1987 Fender were back with a new

Stratocaster, the American Standard, and with it came a re-designed vibrato using a twin-post, knife-edge pivot design. Their Strat Plus added locking tuners and introduced to the market Trev Wilkinson and his "roller nut". This guitar gave massive credibility to the "system" vibrato: bridge unit, friction-reducing nut and locking tuners. In 1990 Wilkinson launched his VS100 vibrato which with Sperzel locking tuners and a friction-reducing nut became one of the most popular systems of the early 1990s.

The Parker Fly, released in 1993, featured a new vibrato with piezo-loaded saddles to give an "acoustic-like" tone. The same technology was also used on Fishman's Powerbridge, a piezo-equipped retrofit vibrato launched in 1995. The following year acoustic pickup manufacturer L.R. Baggs joined the piezo bridge race with the X-Bridge. This like the Powerbridge is designed as a direct retrofit for a Fender American Standard Stratocaster.

(Please note that we use the term "vibrato" throughout this book. You will also hear the device variously called a tremolo, a wang bar, a whammy, and probably quite a few more. We say "vibrato" because that is the technically accurate term.)

Two early types of vibrato are illustrated on the guitars here. Doc Kauffman's crude vibrato is fitted to this 1930s Rickenbacker electric, while the late-1950s Gretsch Chet Atkins (above) has a Bigsby vibrato.

Bigsby The Bigsby offers minimal pitch change, ideal for light vibrato styles. Bigsbys come in various designs to fit archtop, flat-top and semi-hollow designs. They're available as a retrofit (a pro job) and due to their current popularity appear on an increasing number of new instruments. But unlike the combined bridge/tailpiece Strat vibrato, the Bigsby is a vibrato *tailpiece*. Its mechanical success therefore relies on the efficiency of the separate bridge, which often explains the poor accuracy of its return-to-pitch. But of course Bigsbys do *look* good...

Fender vintage-style Strat The key to this bridge's longevity is its versatility. It can be tilted up to create around a tone up-bend and down to quite slack, or – as Clapton uses it – it can be set flat on the body as a fixed bridge. It doesn't have the most efficient pivot system, and the pressed-steel saddles have limited height adjustment with often uncomfortable protruding screws. The arm screws in and is not usually adjustable for swing tension.

Fender American Standard Strat This is a highly successful update of the vintage vibrato. The two-post knife-edge pivot means more efficient tuning stability, and this one can float above the body – or be set like a vintage vibrato/fixed bridge. The solid, compressed-stainless-steel saddles offer more height adjustment and have "hidden" adjusting screws. The screw-in arm comes with a spring that allows better arm placement (an idea that predates this vibrato).

Floyd Rose II This is one of the most common versions of this double-locking design. It floats above the body, which often has a rout at the rear to increase the vibrato's upward travel. The strings lock in the saddles, but the saddle radius is preset at about 406mm (16″). The arm is secured with a screw-on collar and the vibrato's travel is very wide: from totally slack to often a four- or five-semitone up-bend before the strings choke on the frets. For maximum efficiency it should be fitted with a nut lock – but not everyone likes the hassle of string-locks at both nut and saddle.

Ibanez Lo-Pro (Floyd Rose-licensed) This is a typical example of an "improved" Floyd Rose. To maximise tuning stability the two height-adjustable pivot posts have a central-

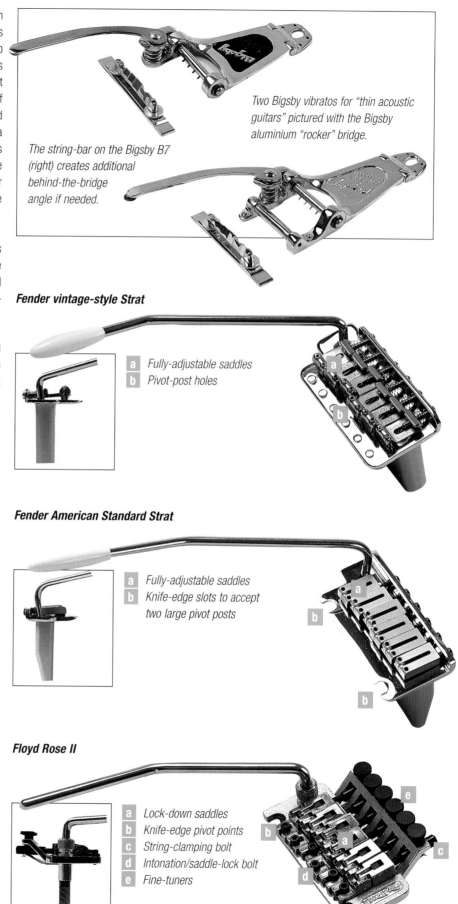

Two Bigsby vibratos for "thin acoustic guitars" pictured with the Bigsby aluminium "rocker" bridge.

The string-bar on the Bigsby B7 (right) creates additional behind-the-bridge angle if needed.

Fender vintage-style Strat

a *Fully-adjustable saddles*
b *Pivot-post holes*

Fender American Standard Strat

a *Fully-adjustable saddles*
b *Knife-edge slots to accept two large pivot posts*

Floyd Rose II

a *Lock-down saddles*
b *Knife-edge pivot points*
c *String-clamping bolt*
d *Intonation/saddle-lock bolt*
e *Fine-tuners*

SETTING STRING HEIGHT

Tune-o-matic Overall height adjustment on the Tune-o-matic type bridge, for example as fitted by Gibson and Epiphone, is set using a slot-head screw **A** (main picture) or a thumb-wheel **A** (inset). The radius created by the bridge is not adjustable except by notching the saddles, which is a job for a pro.

In order to lower the string height, turn the slot-head screw or thumb-wheel clockwise, and the pitch of the strings will drop slightly. In order to raise the string height you must first slacken the strings to achieve any upward movement. Then turn the bridge's screw or the thumb-wheel anti-clockwise (counter-clockwise). Tune back to pitch and re-measure. Once you've achieved the correct string height,

check the stud tailpiece. The strings should run from the back of the saddles to the tailpiece without touching the back edge of the bridge **B**. You may need to raise the stud tailpiece, but keep the angle as steep as possible. The adjustment of this tailpiece is the same as for the one-piece wrapover bridge (see next item).

One-piece wrapover Gibson's one-piece wrapover bridge/tailpiece (or any of the variants) has two large slot-head studs which adjust the string height. (Like the Tune-o-matic, the radius of the bridge is preset.) It's doubtful you'll have a big enough screwdriver – and don't use one with a blade width that's smaller than the stud slot because you'll damage the stud. Instead, slacken off the

string tension and you may find you can simply move the studs by hand (or with the aid of a stiff plectrum or two or a small coin placed in the slot).

A tip passed on by top UK luthier Sid Poole is to slacken off the string tension and place a piece of paper towel over the slot and insert the curved end of your 6″ steel rule **C**. Note that the edges of these rules can be very sharp – you may want to wrap a piece of kitchen paper around the rule. The pro tool for the job is Stewart-MacDonald's Stop Tailpiece Post Wrench (see p18). Make a turn on the bass stud, then the treble. Tune up and re-measure your string height. Take your time otherwise you'll damage those stud slots. And don't forget, *always slacken the string tension before adjusting these studs*.

Other six-saddle types Some six-saddle bridges have height adjustment for each string. For fixed-bridge, six-saddle Tele or Strat bridges, for example, the adjustment is the same as the Stratocaster vibrato bridge (see below). Three-saddle Telecaster bridges don't give as much precise height control as a six-saddle bridge, but by setting the height screw next to each string – so angling the paired bridge saddles – you can achieve the necessary radius.

If you have a bolt-on-neck guitar and for any reason you don't have the necessary range of saddle adjustment available to achieve your desired string height, see neck-pitch adjustment (p31/32).

Vibrato bridges Because the height (and therefore radius) of the saddles on the Floyd Rose is preset, the two height-adjustable pivot posts offer the principal way to adjust string height **D**. To minimise wear it's recommended that you slacken off the string tension before raising/lowering the posts of any floating vibrato. Usually a Floyd Rose has a flat-ish saddle radius of about 406mm (16″). If your fingerboard radius is smaller you'll have to put up with the outer strings being slightly higher than the inner ones in order to avoid fret rattle, so in this case measure your string height firstly from the G-string and D-string, not the outer E-strings. (You can alter the height of a Floyd Rose's saddles with very thin shim steel – try a hardware store. Simply cut some small pieces that will fit under the central saddles and raise their height to create a smaller

A ADJUSTING A TUNE-O-MATIC BRIDGE'S STRING HEIGHT (SLOT-HEAD SCREW TYPE)

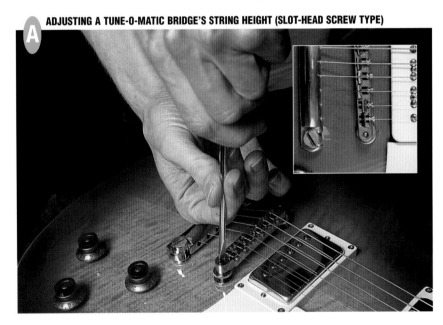

B TUNE-O-MATIC STRING PATH

C WRAPOVER BRIDGE ADJUSTMENT

WHAT IS ACTION?

For many players the "action" of an electric guitar is the height of the strings above the frets, typically measured from the top of the 12th fret to the underside of the outer two strings: the low E (bass) and the high E (treble). If only it were that simple. In reality, action is a general term used to describe the combination of the entire playing "feel" of the guitar. You'll hear comments like, "This guitar has a really low action," or, "The action's really high on this one," and the reasons are not just to do with the physical distance of the strings from the frets. Neck condition is crucial. The neck's straightness and relief, the fingerboard radius in relation to the bridge's saddle radius, and the nut and even fret height all contribute to the player's perception – *your* perception – of

action. For example, as we've considered in Neck (see p32), the relief of the neck will alter the string height.

More relief (concave bow) places the frets further from the strings, and vice versa. Big, high frets often give the impression of a greater string height simply because the fret's top, or playing surface, is further from the face of the fingerboard. Of course, without having your guitar refretted you can't do anything about this yourself. But what you can do, having adjusted the neck, is to set a string height that's most suitable for you.

Many players simply strive for the lowest possible action "without buzzes". As we've already discussed, that may never be achievable – and anyway would not always be the "best" set-up. The best set-up is simply the

one that suits you and that suits your playing style, your instrument, and how often you practise and play.

There is of course an essential element here that we've purposely left to last: your strings. We've already discussed (in Neck, see p26) the effect of different string gauges on the neck itself, as well as the feel of the strings in relation to your guitar's scale length.

But those aspects aside, a heavier gauge will simply feel harder to play, at least at first. Likewise, the higher the string height of your guitar, the tougher the guitar feels to fret and bend. Certainly the additional mass of the heavier gauge should give you a bigger sound, and a higher action should mean a cleaner, less buzzy tone. But it's going to require more physical effort and practice.

A guitar with a low string-height and light-gauge strings will feel fine for bedroom practice. But on-stage, as all that adrenaline pumps through you and naturally makes you play harder, a heavier gauge and possibly higher action may be more suitable. So changing your string gauge is a lot more complex than just re-stringing your guitar.

MEASURING STRING HEIGHT

Assuming that the neck of your guitar is correctly adjusted and that your nut isn't too high or too low, you can now proceed to setting the string height.

• Using a steel ruler, measure the string height of the outer strings at the 12th fret – from the top of the fret to the underside of the string. A basic guide would be about 1.6mm (¹⁄₁₆″) on the treble side (high E) and 2.0mm (⁵⁄₆₄″) on the bass side (low E). (See chart, left.) What about the other strings? They should gradually curve from the height of the low E to the height of the high E, creating a radius that will follow that of the fingerboard. With all the previous considerations taken into account, that'll contribute to a slightly high action, but ideally one that plays cleanly and buzz-free. This is a good starting point.

• To adjust string heights you need to raise or lower the bridge or its individual saddles. If you have a new guitar the chances are you'll have an owner's manual. *Always read this thoroughly!* The most specialist tool you'll need is the *correct* size of Allen key (see Tools p16/17) to set the height-adjustable saddles and some vibrato pivot posts.

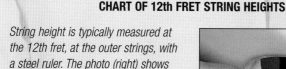

CHART OF 12th FRET STRING HEIGHTS

String height is typically measured at the 12th fret, at the outer strings, with a steel ruler. The photo (right) shows string-height measurement being taken at the bass side.

	12th-fret string-height at treble	12th-fret string-height at bass
LOW	1.2mm (³⁄₆₄″)	1.6mm (¹⁄₁₆″)
MEDIUM	1.6mm (¹⁄₁₆″)	2.0mm (⁵⁄₆₄″)
HIGH	2.0mm (⁵⁄₆₄″)	2.4mm (³⁄₃₂″)
SLIDE	3.2mm (⅛″)	3.6mm (⁹⁄₆₄″)

The above measurements are approximate guides and will depend on string gauge, neck condition and nut height.

locking grub screw, the fine tuners are placed more comfortably behind the saddles, and the push-fit arm has two nylon washers to set a tighter or looser swing.

PRS This fine update of the Fender vibrato attacks all the points that contribute to tuning instability. The six-screw pivot system looks like a vintage Strat but each hole on the bridge plate is honed to a knife-edge and locates into notches on the six fixing screws. The inertia or sustain block has deep drilled holes that reduce the "dead" string length in the block and are believed to add to overall tuning stability, while the stainless steel arm is a push-fit type with tension adjustment. Only available on PRS guitars, the vibrato is part of a system with PRS-designed locking tuners and friction reducing nut.

Wilkinson VS100 Designed as a floating vibrato, this uses distinct oblong-shaped compressed-stainless-steel saddles. Once intonation and height are set the saddles lock down, minimising movement and sustain loss. The string spacing of the current VS100 (made by Gotoh in Japan) is preset by the tracks under each saddle, whereas the original US-made bridge had adjustable string spacing. The stainless steel arm push-fits into a delrin insert in the block and is adjustable for tension. For best results it's used as a system with friction-reducing nut and locking tuners, and can provide wide travel approximating that of a Floyd Rose (but without the locks). The Wilkinson is a highly popular unit due to its availability to any manufacturer or as a retrofit (directly for the Fender American Standard Stratocaster, and with some body modification for a variety of Strat-style guitars). A simpler version, the VS50K, is made under license in Korea and appears on many low-end guitars.

Fishman Powerbridge Originally launched on a Wilkinson VS100, Fishman's Powerbridge uses piezo inserts in the saddles to create an "amplified acoustic" tone. This technology was an off-shoot of the unique Parker Fly "hybrid" guitar (Larry Fishman is president of Parker guitars). A "vintage" version (as pictured, right) is also available as are fixed-bridge versions, and a new non-Wilkinson Powerbridge was launched in 1998. Other manufacturers of piezo-bridges include Mike Christian, L.R. Baggs, Gotoh and Shadow.

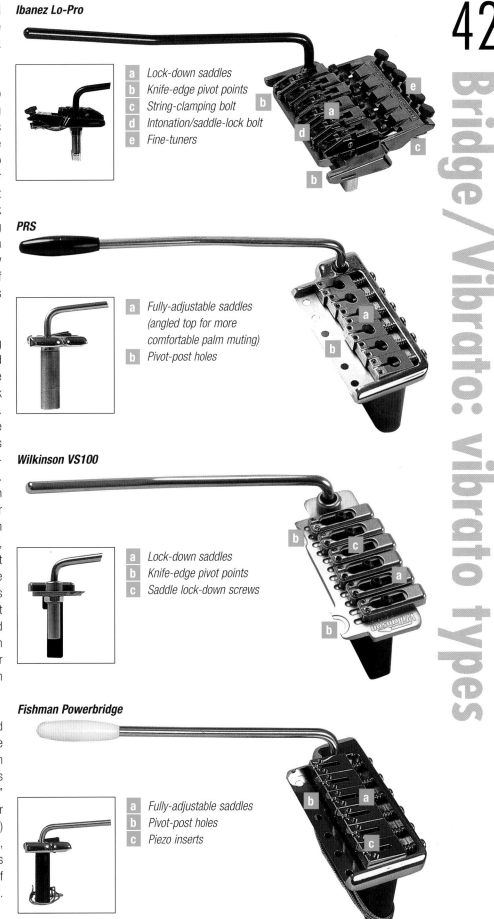

Ibanez Lo-Pro

a Lock-down saddles
b Knife-edge pivot points
c String-clamping bolt
d Intonation/saddle-lock bolt
e Fine-tuners

PRS

a Fully-adjustable saddles (angled top for more comfortable palm muting)
b Pivot-post holes

Wilkinson VS100

a Lock-down saddles
b Knife-edge pivot points
c Saddle lock-down screws

Fishman Powerbridge

a Fully-adjustable saddles
b Pivot-post holes
c Piezo inserts

D ADJUSTING FLOYD ROSE PIVOT POSTS

E ADJUSTING STRAT SADDLES

F USING A RADIUS GAUGE

G ADJUSTING WILKINSON PIVOT POSTS

H ADJUSTING WILKINSON SADDLES

radius with a higher "arch".) A Strat – especially a Strat with a vibrato – is more complex as it has six saddles, each adjustable for height, usually with an Allen key **E**. Having set the outer two strings for height, use the steel rule to measure the inner four, gradually increasing height from treble to bass strings.

As we've said, if you have a vintage-style Fender with small fingerboard radius (184mm/7¼″) you may encounter upper-fret choking (strings hitting frets when you play). So once the string height is set, try some upper-fret bends. If the string chokes on a higher fret, raise the saddle further.

You may find that using a radius gauge **F** (available from Stewart-MacDonald, or you can make one yourself) is a more convenient way to match the radius of the saddles to the radius of the fingerboard once the outer two string-heights have been set. Current Fender US and Mexican guitars have a 241mm (9½″) fingerboard radius, while Japanese Strat reissues (and some older-style US models) have a smaller 184mm (7¼″) radius.

Using a radius gauge is a fine starting point, but as usual it's worth remembering that there are no "correct" settings. Once you've set the saddle radius you may, for example, want to reduce slightly the height of the centre strings – but you must retain a gentle curve.

Alternatively, you can set the string height of any multi-saddle bridge totally by "feel". Simply lower each string until you get continuous buzzing on most frets, then raise it gradually until most of the buzzes disappear.

On Wilkinson's VS100 you can adjust both the pivot-post height and the individual saddle height. Basically, the pivot posts are for setting the overall string height **G**, and the individual saddles **H** help to match the fingerboard radius. *Before making any height or intonation adjustments on a Wilkinson vibrato, slacken off the saddle lock-down screw.* The outer saddles should start flat on the vibrato baseplate. Then turn the pivot posts clockwise, lowering the vibrato until the outer strings just touch the highest fret. You can then alter the heights of the other saddles to just touch that last fret, thereby perfectly matching your fingerboard radius. Now raise the pivot posts until you achieve the correct string height. This works with Fender's American Standard Strat vibrato too, although the base of the outer saddles should sit approx 2.4mm (³⁄₃₂″) from the face of the baseplate.

VINTAGE-STYLE STRAT VIBRATOS

The vintage-style Strat vibrato pivots on its six front-mounted screws, and does not float above the body like a Floyd Rose or Wilkinson vibrato. Therefore the back of this Strat vibrato usually tips up to create up-bend. But you can, for example, have the vibrato set flat on the body so you only have down-bend, with the advantage that if you break one string the others won't go out of tune. Another option is to make the guitar into a totally non-vibrato instrument by setting the vibrato hard down on the body and leaving the arm in the case.

Achieving different set-ups is relatively easy. Basically, the strings' tension is counteracted by the tension on the two (or more) springs in the vibrato cavity in the rear of the body. Remove the vibrato backplate and you'll see that the springs are hooked at one end onto the vibrato's sustain block and at the other onto the spring "claw". This claw is held to the body with two cross-head screws. The number of springs (and their combined tension) plus the distance of the spring claw from the neck-facing end of the spring cavity will affect the position of the vibrato.

The number and type of springs you fit will affect not only the overall tension but also the feel of the vibrato. Three springs with .010″ gauge strings on a Strat is pretty standard. Drop down to two springs and the vibrato feels lighter and its return-to-pitch can be less stable. With lighter .009″ gauge strings and two springs it usually feels very smooth, but the firmer feel of three springs is often preferred. Heavier-gauge strings need more springs, and if you want to defeat the action of the vibrato so it sits flat and tight on the body, put all five in. Remember, the "correct" setting of the vibrato is always a balance between strings and springs.

It's worth pointing out that, because of this string-to-spring balance, a Strat vibrato (or indeed any vibrato based on this principle) has limitations. If you bend one string, the rest go flat (try it). You have to bend the string further to achieve the same degree of pitch change as you would on an equivalent fixed-bridge guitar. Country-style bends become tricky too. You may bend one string upwards while fretting and voicing another string... and the un-bent string will go flat. Products like the Fender/Hipshot Trem-setter and WD's Tremolo Stabiliser aim to reduce this problem, but they are not easy to set up and you'll need a pro's

VINTAGE-STYLE STRAT VIBRATO SET-UP

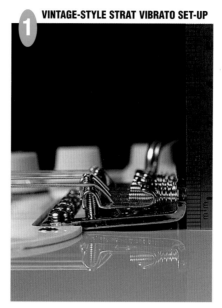

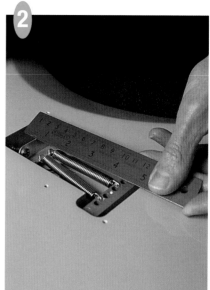

help. If this type of bending is important to your style you may want to consider a fixed-bridge guitar or set the Strat vibrato flat on the body so it doesn't move.

Different springs vary in tension. Combine this with how you like your vibrato to feel and there really are no set rules. So long as the set-up works for you and stays pretty much in tune, then that's the right one.

Typically, however, a vintage Strat vibrato is set so that there is a gap of approximately 2mm-3mm (⁵⁄₆₄″-⅛″) between the back of the bridge and the face of the guitar. This should give an up-bend of approximately one semitone on the top E-string and around a tone on the low E-string, assuming that .009″-.042″ gauge strings are fitted.

VINTAGE-STYLE STRAT VIBRATO SET-UP

1 Assess your existing set-up. Measure the height of the tip-up angle – if there is one – at the back of the bridge (pictured). Remove the backplate cover and check the springs. For a lighter feel, use two springs set from the sustain block's outer holes to the spring claw's two inner hooks. For a firmer feel, use one more spring from the block's central hole to the claw's central hook. Move the springs one at a time if necessary; lift off the springs at the block first, then hook them onto the claw and reposition the other end into the block.

2 The length of the spring cavity differs between Strat models, and of course springs (and strings) vary in tension. So there is no one set position for the spring claw. However, to give you an idea of how it moves, I measured my Fender reissue Strat (pictured) fitted with a set of .009"-.042" gauge strings. The spring claw with three springs measured approximately 16mm (⅝") from the neck-facing edge of the back cavity to the neck-facing edge of the claw, and when fitted with two springs measured 9mm-10mm (about ⅜"). If you're using .010"s you're better off with three springs – I set the claw 13mm-14mm (½"-⁹⁄₁₆") from the cavity edge. Make sure the claw is parallel to the neck-facing edge of the cavity.

3 Tune to pitch. Measure the height of the tip-up angle and adjust *both* the spring-claw screws. If you need more tip-up angle

undo (turn anti/counter-clockwise) the two claw screws (pictured). Start with two full turns per screw and keep the spring claw parallel with the cavity. Tune the guitar back to pitch and re-measure the up-tilt. If you've gone too far, *tighten* both screws; on the other hand, if you need more tip-up, *loosen* the screws. After every small adjustment it's important to re-tune to pitch and then re-measure the up-tilt. When you've got about 2.5mm (³⁄₃₂") of tip-up angle, check the amount of up-bend. You should find, with the vibrato pulled all the way up, that you have about a one-semitone up-bend on the top E-string, that the low E-string will easily rise by two or maybe even three semitones, and that you can achieve around a tone up-bend on your G-string. You can

precisely tune this up-bend by adjusting the spring claw screws.

4 Now check the position of the six pivot screws at the front of the bridge. Undo the centre four screws a couple of full turns so they sit slightly above the vibrato. Hold the vibrato flat down on the body with the vibrato arm and screw the two outer screws down (not overtight) onto the bridgeplate (pictured). Release the vibrato arm and unscrew the outer screws until they just clear the top of the plate after the vibrato has rested in its angled position. If you've already set your action (string) height (see p43-45), then all you need to do is just re-check it. You're now ready to set your intonation (see p48/49) and maximise tuning stability (see p51 and p53).

PRO'S PERSPECTIVE: BLOCK VOTE

A Fender vibrato tip handed on from British luthier Phil Norsworthy (and used by Fender, as reported by Dan Erlewine in the "Guitar Player Repair Guide") is to use a small tapered wooden block that you place in the rear vibrato cavity between the back of the vibrato's sustain block and the cavity. Because of the block's taper, it allows you to set the precise position of the floating vibrato. With the block in place, slacken off the spring tension so that the string tension holds the block. Now you can make your adjustments to string-height, radius and intonation without the vibrato moving. Once

set, tighten the spring claw (above). Keep it parallel, and when it's tight enough the block literally just drops out, leaving you with the vibrato perfectly set and in-tune. These time-saving tapering blocks can also be used on

numerous other floating or vintage-style vibratos, although the precise size of the block's tapering thickness will vary according to the vibrato type and the size of the rear spring cavity. For Floyd Rose vibratos which usually float parallel to the face of the guitar, Norsworthy recommends a block 36mm x 25mm (1½" x 1"), tapering from 16mm to 12mm (⅝" to ½"). For Fender American Standard guitars which usually have a slight tip-up angle of between 2.4mm (³⁄₃₂") and 3mm (⅛"), Fender themselves use a block 50mm x 25mm (2" x 1") that tapers from around 12mm to 6mm (½" to ¼").

SETTING UP TWO-SCREW FLOATING VIBRATOS

Floating vibratos like the Floyd Rose, Wilkinson and the type fitted to the modern Fender American Standard Strat all work on the same principle employed on the vintage vibrato: that is, the string tension is balanced by the spring tension. However, they use a more efficient pivot point in the form of two height-adjustable posts, and they "float" parallel to the face of the guitar. (Note that the American Standard vibrato can float parallel or be set like a vintage vibrato, although you will probably need to adjust the neck pitch to alter the set-up.)

To set these vibratos to the correct position, use the same method described for the vintage-style vibrato on these pages, but

instead of measuring just the back of the bridge, measure both the distance of the underside of the bridge to the face of the body at the front of the bridge, and then again the distance at the back of the bridge.

For optimum performance these two measurements should be the same. The distance from the front of the bridge to the body directly affects action height: adjust the spring tension to equalise the distance at the front and back of the bridge. For maximum pivot efficiency, make sure both pivot posts are adjusted to virtually the same height.

Two floating vibratos (right: Wilkinson, top; Peavey Floyd Rose, below) showing the "gap" between the vibrato's base and the body.

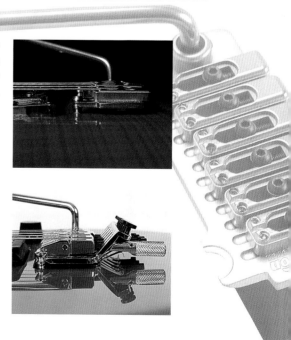

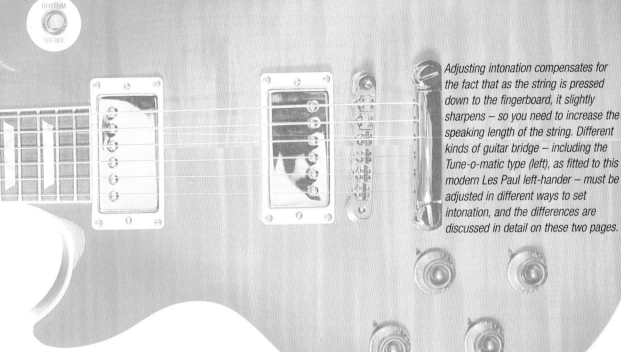

Adjusting intonation compensates for the fact that as the string is pressed down to the fingerboard, it slightly sharpens – so you need to increase the speaking length of the string. Different kinds of guitar bridge – including the Tune-o-matic type (left), as fitted to this modern Les Paul left-hander – must be adjusted in different ways to set intonation, and the differences are discussed in detail on these two pages.

ADJUSTING INTONATION

We've discussed the reason for intonation adjustments in the Neck section earlier. The making and checking of any such adjustments is crucial. Also, whenever you change string gauge (or indeed brand) you must re-check your intonation.

Fine-tuning the intonation, especially with individually adjustable saddles, is fairly straightforward – but you'll need an electronic tuner. The bridge or vibrato, string height, truss rod and nut height should be properly set up before you set the intonation, and ideally the frets should be in good condition. Here is the basic procedure for setting the intonation on all guitars, except those fitted with a nut lock, for which see the scheme for Floyd Rose-style vibratos (p50/51).

• Tune strings to pitch and sound the 12th fret harmonic of the first string. Now, compare this with the note produced by fretting the same string at the 12th fret.
• If the fretted note is sharp compared to the harmonic, the string length must be increased by moving the saddle away from the neck.
• If the fretted note is flat the saddle must be moved forwards, towards the neck, shortening the string length. You can remember this by the simple phrase: "Fret, Flat, Forward." This should help you recall that if the *fretted* note is *flat*, move the string saddle *forward* towards the neck. Just remember the three Fs: Fret, Flat, Forward.
• Repeat this procedure, on all strings, until the harmonic and the fretted notes are the same.

A **INTONATION ADJUSTMENT ON TUNE-O-MATIC BRIDGE**

B **INTONATION ADJUSTMENT ON STRATOCASTER BRIDGE**

PRO'S PERSPECTIVE: TUNING HELL

The Hellcasters' Jerry Donahue is very particular when it comes to setting-up his guitars. Over the years he's evolved a very neat method not only solving the problems of a three-saddle Telecaster bridge but also, Jerry believes, making any guitar with a six-saddle bridge play more in-tune. Here's how he sets his three-saddle Telecasters.

• Tune all open strings as normal. But set the centre saddle so that the G-string fretted at the 12th fret is marginally sharp of its harmonic (which is in tune). The D-string fretted at the 12th is therefore marginally flat of the harmonic.

• Now, using the tuner, adjust the G-string so that you get that fretted note in tune, effectively flattening the G-string. A root-position E-major chord should sound in-tune to your ear, with the G-sharp (first fret G-string) slightly flat, but not so much that a root-position E-minor chord sounds out.

• Jerry finds that the top strings are usually fairly in-tune, but sets the B-string fretted at the 12th very slightly sharp of the harmonic; the top E-string fretted at the 12th and its harmonic should be the same.

• On the low E- and A-string saddle, Jerry sets the A in tune – fretted at the 12th and the harmonic. Again, he finds the difference here is almost always minimal; he usually flattens the low E very slightly anyway.

INTONATION ADJUSTMENT ON WRAPOVER BRIDGE

INTONATION ADJUSTMENT ON TELECASTER BRIDGE

INTONATION AND BRIDGE TYPES

Thc intonation adjustments described on the opposite page are usually made with a Phillips (cross-head) screwdriver or with an Allen key. But note that Gibson's Tune-o-matic bridge **Ⓐ** (and the various versions thereof) is a notable exception that is typically adjusted for intonation by way of slot-head screws.

• Bear in mind, once again, that you must slacken the string tension before you start to move an individual saddle away from the bridge, especially on Fender-style Strat **Ⓑ** and Tele bridges, although this also applies to the various brands and varieties of one-piece combination bridge/tailpieces.

• Always have new strings fitted, and don't have the pickups too close to the strings, especially the neck pickup, as the magnetic pull will interfere with string vibration and distort the pitch.

On bridges such as the one-piece wrapover type **Ⓒ**, with overall intonation adjustment, you use the small grub screws that protrude from the back of the bridge to set that overall intonation. Here you need only check the outer strings; the angled position of the bridge itself allows a basic compensation for the rest. You may find that setting the bass-side intonation using the D-string, rather than the low E-string, sounds more accurate.

Similarly, on a three-saddle Telecaster bridge **Ⓓ** you can only set the intonation per *pair* of strings.

If you start by intonating the first paired saddle to the top E-string, the theoretical result is that the fretted B-string will sound sharp at the 12th fret compared to its harmonic there. If you find the B-string too sharp when you come to play chords in high-fret positions, then move the saddle backwards a little. This will bring the B-string more in tune, but make the top E-string slightly flat.

On the middle G-string/D-string saddle, if you use the D-string to set the intonation, the G-string will probably end up sharp. Again, you can always move the saddle backwards a little to improve this string, but this will in turn make the D-string slightly flat.

These compromise settings are inevitable and will be magnified by all the factors that affect intonation such as string gauge and action height. (Also see the Pro's Perspective: Tuning Hell at the top of this page.)

ADJUSTING INTONATION ON FLOYD ROSE-STYLE VIBRATO BRIDGES

Setting intonation on a guitar with a double-locking Floyd Rose-style vibrato is complex and it's best to get the job done professionally. If you want to try it yourself here's what to do.

• Unlock the three locking bolts at the locking nut **A**.

• Compare the 12th fret harmonic with the note at the 12th fret.

• Remember: if the fretted note is flat, compared to the harmonic, the string length is too long, so the saddle needs to be moved closer to the neck; conversely, if the fretted note is sharp, the string length is too short, so the saddle needs to be moved further away from the neck.

• Slacken off the individual string tension and visualise the position of the saddle. Undo the saddle lock with the correct Allen key while holding the saddle-locking bolt with your spare hand **B**. Only undo the saddle-locking screw enough to move the saddle either slightly forward or slightly backward as required, and no more than about 1.0mm (³⁄₆₄") in the appropriate direction.

• Having made your adjustment, lock down the saddle-locking bolt and re-tune the string. Re-check the intonation and if it is not correct make further adjustments as described.

• When you've completed this for each string, re-check your tuning (see Floyd Rose vibrato tuning, opposite) and don't forget to re-clamp the nut lock.

FLOYD ROSE TIPS

The Floyd Rose may be less fashionable than it once was, but for wide-travel, in-tune bending it takes some beating. As we've discussed, setting intonation is complex and can be time-consuming, as can re-stringing, but the overall set-up is pretty straightforward.

String loading When you're fitting strings on a Floyd Rose vibrato bridge, don't over-tighten the saddle locks **C**. You'll get a feel for the "correct" tightness after a while, and if serious problems occur you should be able to track down replacement saddles from the instrument's manufacturer.

Make sure you always carry in your case or gigbag a good quality pair of wire cutters (and spare strings!) so that prior to loading in the saddle you can cut off the ball-end on the

A ADJUSTING NUT LOCKING BOLTS

B UNDOING THE SADDLE LOCK

C LOADING A STRING

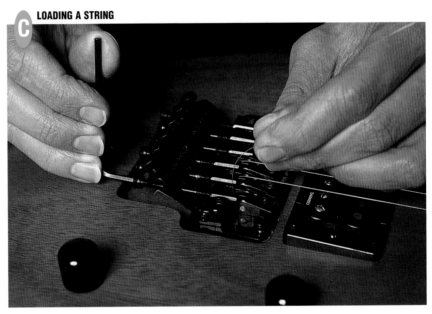

D SADDLE SINGERS INSERT

E STRING-RETAINER BAR

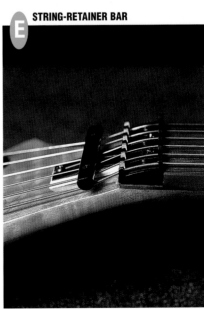

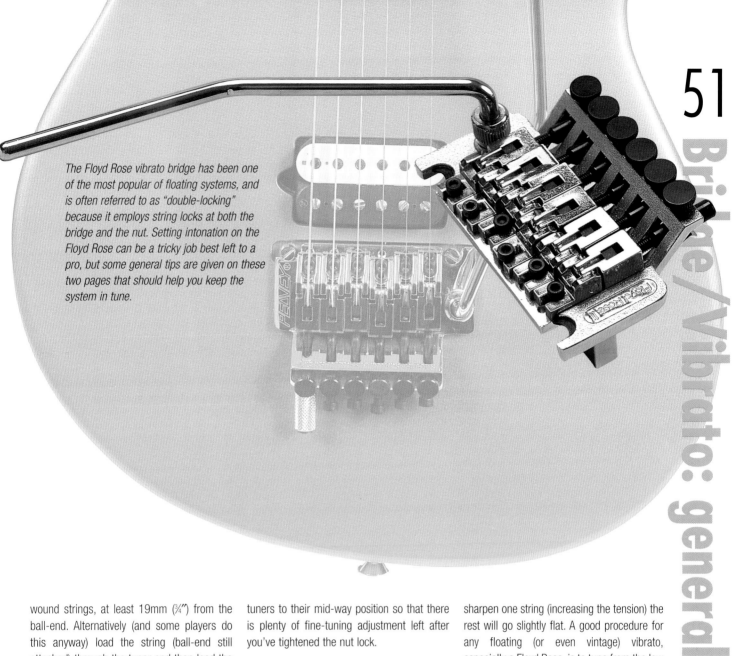

The Floyd Rose vibrato bridge has been one of the most popular of floating systems, and is often referred to as "double-locking" because it employs string locks at both the bridge and the nut. Setting intonation on the Floyd Rose can be a tricky job best left to a pro, but some general tips are given on these two pages that should help you keep the system in tune.

wound strings, at least 19mm (¾") from the ball-end. Alternatively (and some players do this anyway) load the string (ball-end still attached) through the tuner and then load the plain end into the saddle. This method is used by some players who suffer string breakages at the saddle. You can unwind some of the spare string that has wrapped around the tuner post, and in this way you'll give yourself enough extra length to re-fit the old string into the saddle.

Speaking of string breakage, a UK company markets neat Saddle Singers **D** inserts for Floyd Rose-type vibratos, and they're recommended. These prevent saddle wear, which can lead to premature string breakage, and cure string seating problems, benefiting tone. They're easy to fit when you're changing strings – the photo shows one in position at a saddle and with the string ready to load.

Whenever you're replacing one or all of your strings, remember to "centre" the fine-tuners to their mid-way position so that there is plenty of fine-tuning adjustment left after you've tightened the nut lock.

String-retainer bar An often misunderstood feature of the Floyd Rose system is the string-retainer bar **E** situated behind the nut lock. Because the surface of the nut lock is slightly curved, it's important that the string lays flat over the curve, otherwise you will find that when the nut lock is tightened the strings will go noticeably sharp.

Visually check that, once threaded under the retainer bar, the strings sit flat over the nut lock. If they don't, then screw down the string-retainer's screws. Now, if any of these screws should feel tight as you screw down, don't force them. Instead, you should first try removing them and applying a little candle wax to them for lubrication.

Vibrato tuning Tuning any vibrato can be problematic for the simple reason that as you

sharpen one string (increasing the tension) the rest will go slightly flat. A good procedure for any floating (or even vintage) vibrato, especially a Floyd Rose, is to tune from the low E-string first. When that's in tune, go to the A-string. With that one tuned go back to the low E-string, then the A-string again. Only then go to the D-string. With that tuned, return and re-check the previous strings, and carry on using this repetitive back-and-forth procedure.

As with any vibrato it's advisable – even if you're replacing all your strings – to change them one at a time. If you do want to remove all the strings, place a vibrato backplate and/or some stiff card between the back of the vibrato and the face of the guitar to stop the springs pulling the vibrato back. Otherwise the vibrato can come off its pivot points. This is not only inconvenient but can lead to unnecessary wear at these important places.

Finally, having made all your adjustments on the Floyd Rose, you should always remember to tighten the nut locks.

A Bigsby vibrato can be a stylish addition to an instrument, but comes with its own set of problems, including pitch instability.

BIGSBY TIPS

One of the many designs that has re-appeared in the retro-influenced 1990s is the Bigsby vibrato. Originally fitted from the 1950s on Gibsons, Gretsches and even Fender Teles, for example, the Bigsby is a rather archaic pitch-bending device that adds as much to the visual appeal of your guitar as it does to your bag of sonic techniques.

The design is simple, yet the large tailpiece to which the strings anchor overshadows the fact that the travel is minimal – around a semitone up or down. Guitars equipped with Bigsbys are notorious for poor pitch stability, although usually it's not so much the actual tailpiece that's at fault as the nut and bridge.

Many modern guitars fitted with Bigsbys – such as Epiphone's Les Pauls and Washburn's "P" series solidbodies – come with Tune-o-matic-style bridges, as well as large back-angled headstocks where the strings splay out considerably, creating a steep angle over the nut and therefore more chance of strings hitching in their slots.

Tune-o-matic bridges can be retrofitted with Graph Tech friction-reducing saddles, or you can fit a new roller bridge as made by German company ABM, for example.

The nut must be carefully cut: again, a friction-reducing material is ideal. But both jobs are for a pro. However, you might cure minor problems by careful string-loading at the tuners, extensive string-stretching, and lubrication of the nut and saddles. Ultimately, don't forget that the Bigsby is intended for light use. Treat it with respect!

PRO'S PERSPECTIVE: BILL'S BIGSBYS

Changing strings on a Bigsby vibrato can be a fiddly, frustrating job. Bill Puplett, one of the UK's leading repairmen, has the following tips. "You'll find that pre-bending the ends of the new strings to approximately match the diameter of the string-retaining roller-bar helps, especially with the Bigsby models B5, B7 and B12 that feature a secondary hold-down roller-bar. Use any cylindrical-shape object which has a similar diameter to the retaining roller bar, for example a pen or piece of dowel. Hold the ball-end flat against the object and firmly wrap the end of the string about one full turn **Ⓐ**, *then release it. This will produce a hook-shaped curve at the end of the string.*

"Pass this end under the hold-down bar from the bridge side before attaching the ball-end to the retainer pin **Ⓑ**. *You'll notice how the pre-bent string-end makes for easy fitting to the pin and also helps prevent the ball-end coming off the pin while you're installing the other end of the string to the tuner.*

"Make sure the string is properly attached to the tuner's string-post (see Strings p20-23) and tune up so the string has just a bit of tension – don't tune to pitch at this stage. Repeat the bending and installation for the other strings, and then check the string alignment from the retainer bar through to the bridge. Aim to get the strings evenly spaced and running in as straight a line as possible, and make any repositioning adjustments before tuning to pitch. Check the main string-tension spring is properly seated in the top and bottom housings, and then tune to pitch, gently stretching-in the strings as you do so. It also helps to apply some thorough sharp and flat vibrato with the arm, to help the new strings settle.

"When the strings are tuned to pitch, the vibrato arm should come to rest approximately 25mm (1") clear of the pickguard or face of the guitar. This clearance can be adjusted by adding or removing the fibre-disc spacers at the base of the main spring housing. You can use washers of the appropriate size as an alternative, but make sure any spacers are set below the height of the flange which holds the spring in place.

"The Bigsby vibrato is designed to allow a moderate pitch change of around a semitone in either direction. Excessive pitch-changing will inevitably lead to unstable tuning.

"As with most vibrato systems, friction is the main cause of tuning problems; the incorporation of such things as roller or low-friction saddles, a rocker-type bridge, a low-friction nut and so on will greatly aid tuning stability."

Ⓐ BIGSBY: BENDING STRING PRE-LOADING

Ⓑ LOCATING BALL-END; STRING UNDER BAR

KEEPING YOUR VIBRATO IN TUNE

Don't consider any vibrato bridge in isolation. The problem of the vibrato returning all the strings to pitch after use is invariably down to a combination of factors. It's not always the vibrato bridge or tailpiece that is the main culprit; more often it's the points beyond the bridge. The nut, string trees and tuners – and the way you attach your strings – create the major problem, which is friction. The Floyd Rose vibrato system, by locking the strings at the nut and saddle, not only eliminated any friction points but also the effect of the "dead" string length (that is the portion of the string behind the nut and behind the saddle – within, for example, the sustain block of a Strat vibrato).

TUNERS & STRING-STRETCHING

Having set up your vibrato as described you should note once again how careful you must be not to overwind the string around the tuner's string- post. Untidy wraps here will be a major problem. Likewise, no vibrato, not even a Floyd Rose, will return to correct pitch unless you've extensively stretched your strings (see Strings p23).

On a Strat, for example, not only should you stretch the full length of the string between the saddle and the nut, but also make sure you bend the strings behind the nut. This should show up any other problems caused by the string trees and the nut itself.

• If you have tension-adjustable tuners, tighten the screws at the end of the button so the action of the tuner feels tight but not too stiff.

STRING TREES

On a Strat, for example, you'll have one or two string trees of varying design. Not only can the tree itself cause the string to hitch up, but if the tree(s) sit(s) too low on the headstock then the behind-the-nut angle will be too steep and, even with the best cut nut slot, the string may hitch in the nut. Graph Tech make excellent friction-reducing string trees which are inexpensive. They are moulded to include a spacer, giving plenty of height (and therefore a shallow behind-the-nut string angle).

Should the string angle be too shallow – you'll hear a slight buzzing and consequent loss of tone on the open strings if this is the case – you can simply rub the string tree over a piece of medium abrasive paper laid on a flat surface in order to reduce its height. You may be able to remove the G-string/D-string tree altogether, but adding a couple more winds on the string-post when you attach the G-string to the tuner will increase the back-angle and, if this job is done neatly, it shouldn't create any slippage problems.

The best solution for problems with tuners and string trees is to replace your tuners with locking types such as those made by Sperzel, Gotoh and Schaller. The Sperzel Trim-lok tuner, for example, comes with three different post heights so that the behind-the-nut string angle is nicely graduated – and you shouldn't need string trees at all. Tuner replacement is best left to a pro. While it's also a pro job to sort out a nut, you can apply some useful lubricant (soft pencil lead) in the nut slots and under the strings where they pass over the nut.

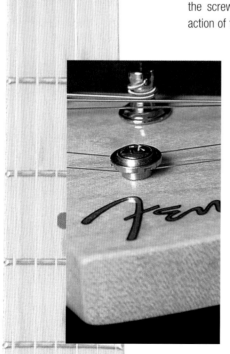 

String trees are usually present on Strat headstocks, and are intended to increase the behind-the-nut string angle of the B-string and high E-string. However, they can also cause either or both strings to hitch in the nut. Shown in the pictures (left) are Fender's vintage-style tree (far left) and Graph Tech's friction-reducing type (near left).

VINTAGE STRAT VIBRATO TIPS

The vintage-style Strat vibrato has caused many problems and provoked much debate over the years. The pivot points of most modern vibratos of this type have been improved. For example, the underside of the bridgeplate holes are usually countersunk to provide a better, more knife-edge-like pivot against the six screws. Lubrication of these points has little lasting effect and should be unnecessary. However, check for noticeable wear on the screws and bridgeplate – and if necessary replace any worn parts.

The vintage-type Strat vibrato has additional friction points both at the saddle and at the point where the string passes over the baseplate on its way to the saddle. Wear on the pressed-steel saddles can cause friction points – especially on the low wound strings – but with a small needle-file and abrasive paper you can smooth these if necessary. Alternatively, if you retrofit friction-reducing saddles these can help both tuning problems and premature string breakages.

Stevie Ray's insulation wire A tip from Stevie Ray Vaughan's guitar tech was to slip over plastic wire insulation **A** at the point where the string bends over the block, to prevent breakage. (The insulation is shown in position in photo **B**.) You can certainly try this.

Solder wrap Tinning (soldering) the wrap at the ball-end of your plain strings is easy to do **C** and will prevent the wrap coming undone with extreme vibrato use.

Spring thing Nothing to do with tuning stability but worth considering here is the fact that some players find the screw-in vibrato arms used by Fender (and many other manufacturers) really annoying: the arms either swing loosely, or tighten up in totally the wrong position.

On the Fender American Standard Stratocaster, Fender's simple cure is to fit a small spring in the vibrato arm's hole **D** which keeps the arm in the right position. These springs cost a few pence each (they're available as Fender spares) and will fit virtually any screw-in vibrato arm hole so long as the hole doesn't go right through the block. Also, keep the arm in the vibrato permanently – just swing it to its lowest position before putting the guitar in its case.

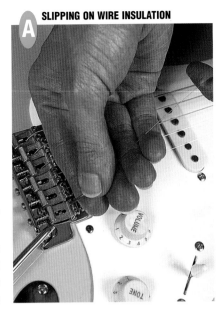

A SLIPPING ON WIRE INSULATION

B WIRE INSULATION IN POSITION

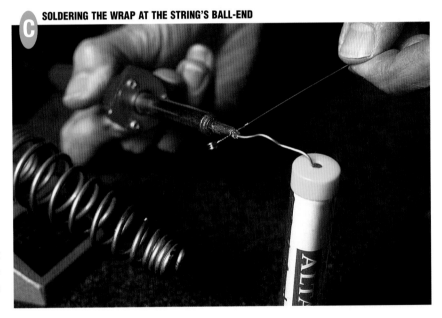

C SOLDERING THE WRAP AT THE STRING'S BALL-END

D FITTING AN ARM-POSITIONING SPRING

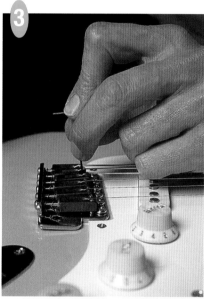

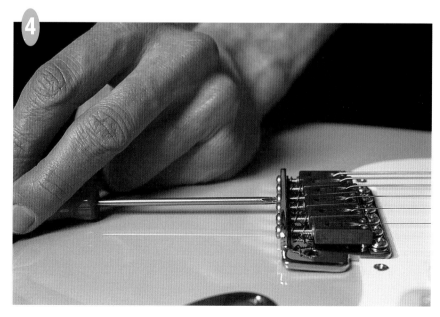

DEALING WITH SADDLE WEAR

As we've already pointed out, your bridge saddles are very important for tone, sustain, intonation and string longevity. The quality of bridge saddles is often overlooked by manufacturers working in the lower price areas because they need to keep down costs, and consequently the materials used often don't maximise such a guitar's performance. Combine that with general wear-and-tear and you have a situation that's far from ideal.

Graph Tech's range of replacement String Saver saddles can provide an easy retrofit answer. They are made of a friction-reducing plastic and should cure any string-hitching problems. They can also maximise string life, and should improve your tone a bit too.

Graph Tech also make a synthetic ivory material called Tusq used for some electric guitar saddles, though mostly for acoustics. These will give a slightly different tone, maximising acoustic resonance and "zing".

Graph Tech's saddles come in a variety of sizes for a variety of guitars, so consult your local store to find the right ones (and remember to take along your guitar). You can easily fit them yourself, and the right time to do this is when you're changing your strings. We fitted them to a Strat, as follows.

1 On Strats and Teles (and other similar guitars) fit one saddle at a time. Remove the first string and unscrew the intonation screw and spring (pictured).

2 Fit the new saddle (pictured) and match its position and height approximately in relation to the other saddles.

3 Fit your new string and adjust the height and intonation (see p48). Do this individually for all the saddles. Then check the string height (pictured).

4 Last, check and if necessary adjust the intonation (pictured).

Tune-o-matic saddle replacements are also available from Graph Tech but not all types are available, and the bridge's saddle screws don't always match the thread of the new saddles (unlike the Strat and Tele types which come with their own new screws). It's really important to get the right ones for your bridge, so replacement here is a little more tricky. Also, the tops of the saddles may need to be notched to achieve the correct string spacing. Consult your store and/or repairman.

HOW A PICKUP WORKS

Up to this point we've looked at the mechanical aspects of the electric guitar – the essential things that make your instrument function correctly before you plug it in. As you'll be aware, unplugged the electric guitar produces only a small amount of acoustic volume when you hit the strings. But it is that small resulting sound – "the singer's voice" – that is sensed by the pickup – "the microphone" – and then increased in volume by your amplifier.

The pickup is a transducer that converts the strings' vibration into electrical voltage which can then be amplified considerably. It's hardly rocket-science. Magnetic pickup designs date back to the 1930s, the industry standard Fender single-coil first appeared on Fender lap-steels in the 1940s, while Gibson's humbucker surfaced in the mid 1950s. And nearly half a decade later it's still these formative designs – namely the single-coil pickup and the humbucking pickup – that dominate the guitars we buy.

Even the way the pickups are controlled on the guitar remains pretty much the same. On a Telecaster, for example, the pickups' signal passes to a simple switch that selects either one or both of the pickups; the signal can then be further manipulated by the volume and tone controls before it reaches the output socket where, thanks to your instrument lead (cord), the signal goes to your amplifier.

Despite numerous attempts by manufacturers to change and update these electronics with more modern technologies, the majority of guitar players are happy with the way it was. What has changed dramatically since the 1950s, however, is our understanding of guitar electronics and the choice of different brands of pickups we can retrofit to alter (and we hope improve) our guitar's tone.

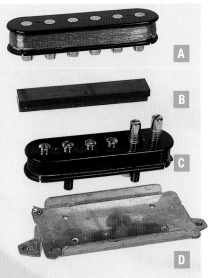

Humbucking pickups use two coils (A,C) mounted over a central magnet (B) onto the baseplate (D). One coil (C) has height-adjustable polepieces; the other (A) has non-adjustable "slug" polepieces.

Plastic cover for single-coil pickup

Bobbin with coil wrap and hook-up wires

Bobbin with "slug" magnets

Pictured is an "exploded" view of a single-coil pickup. The first stage (bottom) shows the staggered-height cylindrical "slug" magnets mounted within the fibre top and bottom plates which form the bobbin. The second stage (centre) shows the same bobbin, now with the coil wire wound around it, and the hook-up cables in place. At the top is the plastic cover which fits over the bobbin for protection.

This photograph shows the electric components and wiring of a Les Paul-style guitar removed and placed on top of the body, with the jack socket and controls below, and the pickups and selector switch to the right. Because in normal circumstances these components are mounted directly to the body, connection and assembly is more elaborate than for Stratocaster-style instruments.

VOLUME & TONE CONTROLS

Under the pickguard, or mounted from the rear of the guitar, the volume control is a simple variable resistor (known as a potentiometer, or pot). As you turn it down – anti-clockwise (counter-clockwise) – it takes the live (hot) output of the pickup and sends it to earth (ground), reducing the output level or volume of the guitar. Another variable resistor, the tone control is usually identical to the volume pot but with an additional small electronic component called a capacitor which as the control is turned down filters off the high frequencies to earth (ground) and makes the sound progressively "darker".

OUTPUT SOCKET (JACK)

In the majority of cases this is a simple mono output connector that takes the live (hot) and earth (ground) signals to your guitar lead (cord). Stereo sockets (jacks), which have two live outputs plus an earth, are used on instruments that may have active electronics and require a battery, and/or on "hybrids" like the Parker Fly where, for example, the magnetic pickup and the piezo pickup outputs can emerge from the guitar separately and be sent to two different amplifiers.

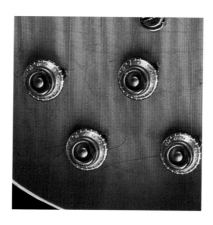

Gibson's four-control layout (left) on a 1960 Les Paul.

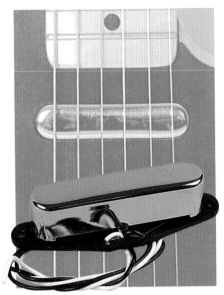

Telecaster-style neck pickup

Telecaster-style bridge pickup

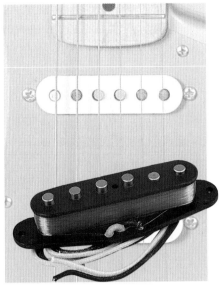

Stratocaster-style staggered-polepiece pickup

Stratocaster-style flush-polepiece pickup

P90-style pickup

Jazzmaster-style pickup

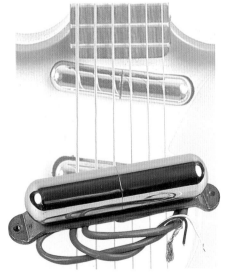

Lipstick-Tube-style pickup

Pictured on this page are some of the main types of single-coil pickups that you will find on your new guitar and/or available as retrofits. Like many aspects of the electric guitar, the choice of new pickups often seems dictated by current music fads and fashions. For example, at the time of writing we're seeing the return to fashion of the Gibson P90-style single-coil which, ironically, originally appeared before both the classic Fender single-coil and the Gibson humbucker.

Shown on the right-hand page are the main types of humbucking pickups to be found on new guitars and/or available as retrofits (top two rows). At the bottom of the page are examples of the newer breed of single-coil-size noise-cancelling pickups. Another fashion note as the electric guitar nears its half-century: the covered humbucker is making a return to favour. A few decades ago players took the covers off their humbuckers in the belief that this improved output and tone.

PICKUP TYPES: Single-coil pickups

This is the simplest type of pickup. The single-coil is used on the majority of Fender Stratocasters and Telecasters, for example, and on the numerous instruments that are made in similar styles.

In its basic form the single-coil pickup consists of six staggered or flush-height alnico rod magnets (magnetic polepieces) around which a coil of fine wire is wound. The slim and quite tall coil of the single-coil and its narrow magnetic field which senses a small part of the vibrating string (the "aperture") account for the single-coil's inherently bright and clear tonality. Two output leads, live (hot) and earth (ground), are connected from the ends of the coil to the control circuitry.

Numerous low-end guitars use a single-coil with chromed steel slugs (non-magnetic polepieces) which connect to one or two ceramic bar magnets on the rear of the pickup. These are cheap, and they can sound harsh and brittle, especially at stage volume.

Humbucker pickups

The humbucker is like two single-coil pickups placed next to each other. Two moulded plastic bobbins have polepieces (height-adjustable, or non-adjustable slug types) around which the coils are wound. The bobbins are mounted over one or two bar magnets (alnico or ceramic), creating opposite magnetic poles at the top of each coil. The two coils are usually wired in "series", and the pickup becomes noise-cancelling or "bucks the hum" (hence the name). This along with the humbucker's wider string-sensing magnetic "aperture" creates the classic humbucker tone, noted for its higher output and typically darker sound than a single-coil. By altering the way in which its coils are linked a humbucker can be wired in "parallel" for a brighter tone with less output while retaining its noise-cancelling properties. Many makers use coil-splitting to "voice" one of the humbucker's two coils, simulating the brighter (non-humbucking) tone of a true single-coil pickup.

Other single-coil types

An increasingly popular single-coil pickup is the P90, which was Gibson's standard guitar pickup before their humbucker was invented. The P90 uses a coil that is wider and less deep than the Fender single-coil, for example, and is noted for its raw, throaty midrange tone.

Another pickup making a return in these retro times is the Lipstick Tube. Another single-coil, it's mounted in what was originally a metal lipstick tube holder. Other classic single-coils include those fitted on Fender Jaguars and Jazzmasters, but with any of these fringe pickup types the choice of replacements is quite limited.

The single-coil-size Fender Lace Sensor pickup works in a slightly different manner, but is still a transducer that converts the strings' energy into electric output. The Lace Sensor comes in various colour-coded types relating to a specific tone/output spec and is used on numerous higher-end Fender guitars. These pickups are noted for quiet performance and a slightly "rounder" top end compared with a good Fender single-coil, making them ideal for higher-gain applications.

Hybrid pickups

The holy grail of pickup design is to achieve true single-coil tone without hum. One relatively new breed of pickup that attempts this is a sort of single-coil/humbucking hybrid, the stacked "single-coil". This is a single-coil-size pickup with two coils stacked on top of one another and that can be wired in series, like a regular humbucker, to create noise-cancelling performance. DiMarzio's Virtual Vintage stacked single-coil pickups, for example, were released in 1997 to great critical acclaim.

Another variant is the side-by-side single-coil-size humbucker. It usually has twin blade polepieces around which two thin coils are wound. Examples include Duncan's Hot Rails and DiMarzio's Fast Track. These "rails" pickups can sound less like single-coils but often offer more power. The advantage of any of these single-coil-size humbuckers is that they will retrofit into a Strat, for example, with virtually no modifications.

The differences between these designs is the subject of much debate among the manufacturers. Seymour Duncan say: "It's easier to use alnico magnets in a stack model, but in our side-by-side single-coil-size pickups we use ceramic to get more magnetic gauss [power] up to the strings. That's probably the biggest difference. For Telecasters we use alnico magnets for 'vintage' tone. For Strats requiring vintage tone and noise-cancelling performance our opinion is that side-by-side humbuckers like our Duck Buckers and

Vintage Rails tend to sound more Stratocaster-like than our Vintage Stack pickup."

Kent Armstrong make a line of pickups in the UK and design the Korean-made Sky pickups. They reckon that side-by-side blade-type pickups tend to sound more compressed and humbucker-like than stack pickups. "The stack still sounds like a single-coil but a little thin in the bass and midrange in comparison," they say. "That's why we don't make stacks."

Seymour Duncan's Little '59 model for Strats and Teles takes one of that maker's most popular full-size humbuckers, the '59, and aims for a similar tone from a single-coil-size package. "It's an approximation, given that the magnetic aperture is around half," say Duncan. "The aperture has an effect primarily in output, but also in other aspects of the sound. The Little '59 in a Tele, say, sounds close to how a full-size humbucker would, but obviously the guitar's construction has a big effect on the overall sound too."

DiMarzio reckon that the side-by-side "single-coil" is lacking in top-end. "It doesn't have the treble burst of energy, because the shape of the magnetic field is so different," they say. "But if you want a pickup with a bigger sound you need a side-by-side. If you increase the magnet size you get more power but more string pull. The full-size humbucker always delivers a lot of power... that's an eight-cylinder engine!"

Active pickups

Active pickups such as EMGs and Duncan's Live Wires are all humbuckers, either full-size side-by-side types or stacked single-coil-size units. Using onboard circuitry (which requires battery power), they create easily the quietest pickups in terms of background noise available anywhere today. They also offer a full range of add-on tone-shaping circuits. Why go active?

"We always equate it to high-quality studios," say EMG. "Most people can relate to the fact that a high quality microphone is going to sound good, and that if you start with a great source you're going to get a pure signal. EMGs are dead quiet and that's ideal for digital recording, but our pickups are simply another colour to paint with. We don't think there is any pickup out there that's the be-all and end-all. Many players' ears are trained to the inconsistency of passive pickups; they prefer them, and that's fine. But a lot of people don't go back once they've heard the difference."

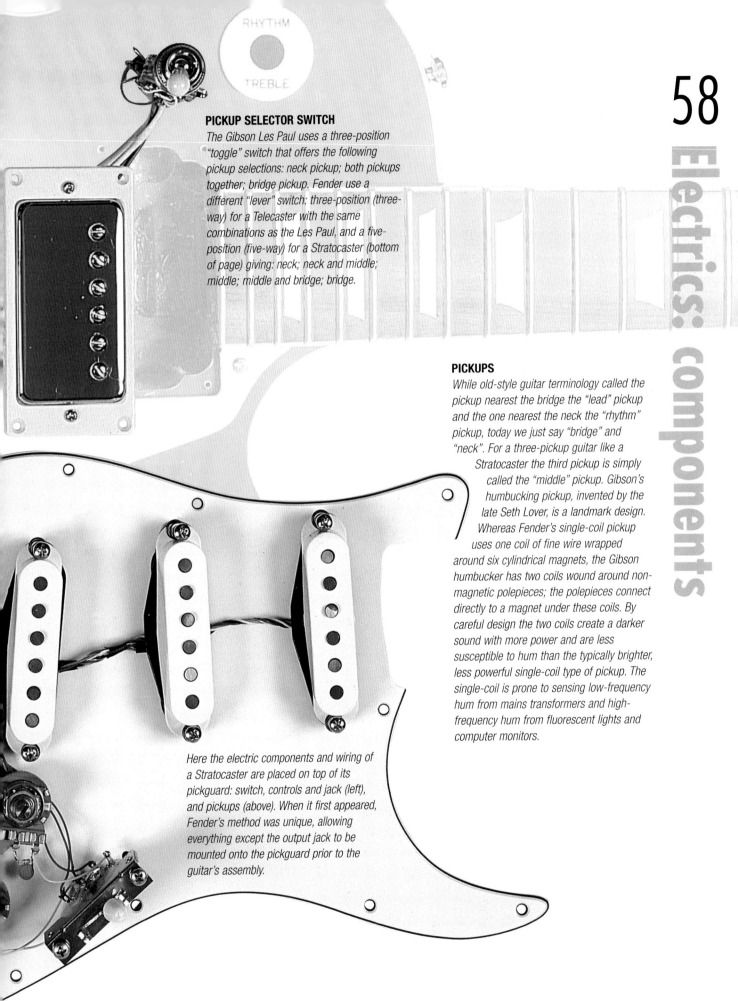

RHYTHM

TREBLE

PICKUP SELECTOR SWITCH
The Gibson Les Paul uses a three-position "toggle" switch that offers the following pickup selections: neck pickup; both pickups together; bridge pickup. Fender use a different "lever" switch: three-position (three-way) for a Telecaster with the same combinations as the Les Paul, and a five-position (five-way) for a Stratocaster (bottom of page) giving: neck; neck and middle; middle; middle and bridge; bridge.

PICKUPS
While old-style guitar terminology called the pickup nearest the bridge the "lead" pickup and the one nearest the neck the "rhythm" pickup, today we just say "bridge" and "neck". For a three-pickup guitar like a Stratocaster the third pickup is simply called the "middle" pickup. Gibson's humbucking pickup, invented by the late Seth Lover, is a landmark design. Whereas Fender's single-coil pickup uses one coil of fine wire wrapped around six cylindrical magnets, the Gibson humbucker has two coils wound around non-magnetic polepieces; the polepieces connect directly to a magnet under these coils. By careful design the two coils create a darker sound with more power and are less susceptible to hum than the typically brighter, less powerful single-coil type of pickup. The single-coil is prone to sensing low-frequency hum from mains transformers and high-frequency hum from fluorescent lights and computer monitors.

Here the electric components and wiring of a Stratocaster are placed on top of its pickguard: switch, controls and jack (left), and pickups (above). When it first appeared, Fender's method was unique, allowing everything except the output jack to be mounted onto the pickguard prior to the guitar's assembly.

Covered humbucking pickup

Filtertron-style pickup

Mini humbucking pickup

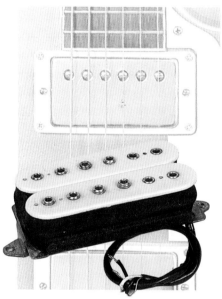

DiMarzio Super Distortion pickup

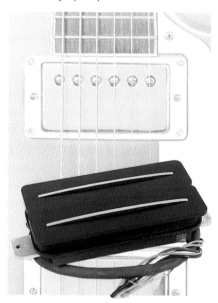

Barden dual-blade humbucking pickup

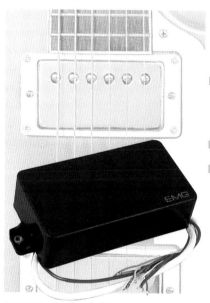

EMG 89 active humbucking pickup

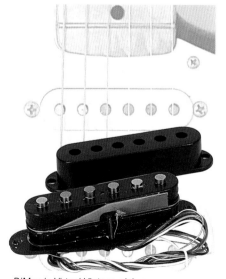

DiMarzio Virtual Vintage pickup

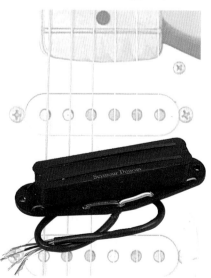

Seymour Duncan Hot Rails pickup

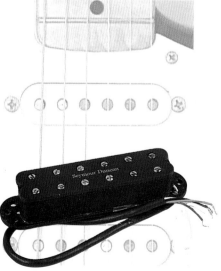

Seymour Duncan Little '59 pickup

Electrics: switches, pots & jacks

PICKUP SWITCHES

Think of a pickup switch as a routing device that selects a pickup before or after the volume control, on its own or in combination with another pickup.

The simplest pickup selector switches are the three-position "toggle" and "lever" types commonly used on two-pickup guitars. Three-pickup guitars like the Stratocaster use a five-way lever switch. Originally, however, they were fitted with just a three-way switch that allowed no combinations of pickups. Players found they could "jam" the switch between positions to create two new sounds, the now famous bridge-and-middle and middle-and-neck combinations.

Occasionally guitar makers use different switches to obtain more complex pickup combinations. For example PRS use a five-position rotary switch to select not only between the instrument's two humbuckers, but also the individual coils within those pickups in both series and parallel combinations. New-generation switches based on the Fender five-way lever type allow similarly complex wiring. Fender's five-way four-pole switch, for example, allows elaborate switching that offers most humbucker and single-coil configurations.

DiMarzio's Steve Blucher utilised a standard two-pole five-way lever switch to create the wiring for Steve Vai's Ibanez JEM guitars, later used for the brand's popular RG Series electrics . Here the switch offers: neck humbucker; bridge-facing single-coil of neck humbucker with mid-placed single-coil; middle single-coil; neck-facing single-coil of bridge humbucker with mid-placed single-coil; bridge humbucker. Gibson's classic Varitone circuit, as used by B.B. King, uses a six-way rotary switch which has various additional components fitted that passively filter the pickups' sound for five tone options (plus a bypass setting).

Smaller "mini-toggle" switches can be used to switch coils in a humbucker. Depending on the outputs from the pickup itself these switches can offer either series or parallel linkage of the two coils and, more usually, switch separate coils on or off (known as coil-splitting or coil-tapping). Technically, a coil-tap refers to a pickup coil which has an additional output lead (the tapped output) at, for example, 75 per cent of its coil winding. This would give a slightly lower and cleaner output than the full coil. Schecter and Tom Anderson guitars use such pickups.

Telecaster/Stratocaster three-way lever switch

Stratocaster five-way lever switch

Toggle switches

Shorter toggle switch for SG-style guitar

Mini-toggle switch

VOLUME & TONE CONTROLS

Volume and tone controls use the same component, a variable resistor called a potentiometer (pot). The value of the potentiometer (its resistance, measured in ohms) affects the eventual tone of the pickup. The majority of guitars with single-coil pickups use a 250k ohm pot; guitars with humbucking pickups use a 500k ohm pot. "A 500k ohm pot keeps the pickup a little brighter," reckon DiMarzio, "and this is most noticeable with the volume full up."

Basically, the higher the pot value the more high-end you'll hear. Consequently some manufacturers prefer 1Meg ohm volume pots for maximum high-end. Pickup maker Seymour Duncan suggest 300k ohm pots. Kent Armstrong say: "Any pickup which has a DC resistance [a measurement often quoted in pickup specs to give an indication of output] of 6k ohms and above needs a 500k ohm pot; anything below works best with a 250k ohm pot." Thus the quoted values of volume and tone pots can be used to subtly "tune" the tone of your pickups.

The difference between a volume and tone pot is that the latter has an additional capacitor (cap). This small component allows high frequencies to pass through but blocks lower frequencies. On a standard tone control the capacitor sends the high frequencies to ground (earth). The value of the capacitor therefore determines how "dark" the tone will become when the control is rotated anti-clockwise (counter-clockwise). Smaller-value capacitors such as those rated at .02 microfarad (abbreviated to µf or mf) allow higher frequencies to pass, and so their effect on a tone control is not as dramatic as, say, a .047mf cap, which would filter more high-end to ground and give a "darker" sound. Some guitar makers like Hamer and Schecter have used a .01mf capacitor on their tone controls to great effect: turned fully anti-clockwise (counter-clockwise) the high-end is only lightly attenuated (reduced in strength).

A smaller-value .001mf capacitor (sometimes with a resistor) is often used, for example on Telecasters and most PRS guitars, between the "in" and "out" contacts of the volume pot to retain high frequencies when the control is turned down. Without this "treble bleed" cap, as you turn down a normal volume pot your high-end tone as well as your volume will be reduced.

The "taper" of a pot determines how smoothly the resistance is applied as the

Jack sockets

control is turned down, and so affects what you'll hear as you alter the controls. Virtually all volume and tone pots used today have logarithmic (audio) as opposed to linear tapers, although some have special tapers specifically suited to guitar use.

A combined volume/tone pot and mini-toggle switch is a useful component, and this "pull/push" type of control means that you can in effect have a mini-toggle switch on your guitar without drilling an additional hole.

The control knob itself should either push-fit onto the splined shaft of the pot or, in the case of Telecaster-type knurled metal control knobs, push-fit over a solid, unsplined shaft where it's held in place by a small set-screw. The threaded sleeve or bushing of a pot (necessary to hold the pot in place with a nut and locking washer) will vary in length. Shorter-sleeve pots are used where the controls are mounted on to the pickguard or control plate (Strats and Teles), but you'll need one with a longer sleeve if you want to retrofit it to a carved-top guitar like a Les Paul or one where the controls mount from the rear through the top of the guitar.

Potentiometer before fitting

Pull/push: combined pot and mini-toggle

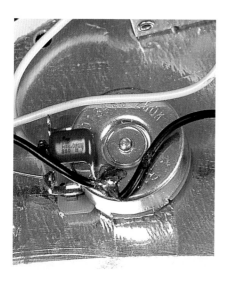

Tone pot, in position in guitar circuit

Volume pot, in position in guitar circuit

ELECTRIC MAINTENANCE

There is a big distinction between the acoustic and electric "sides" of your guitar. The acoustic side of the instrument includes all the factors covered so far: the neck, the truss-rod and the hardware, and how each part is adjusted. Now that we've taken care of the acoustic side, we can move to the maintenance and adjustment of the electric side – as well as looking later at retrofit pickups and wiring modifications.

PICKUP HEIGHT

There are a couple of adjustments to pickups that can improve and balance the guitar's output. Both single-coils and humbuckers have overall height adjustment for the whole unit. The closer the pickup is to the strings the more output you'll get, and vice-versa. If the pickup is too close to the strings, however, problems can occur with the magnetic pull of the pickup or, in the worse case, the strings can actually collide with the pickup, stopping them dead. Here's what you do.

• Fret the outer strings (one at a time) at the top fret (21st, 22nd or 24th). Measure the distance from the top of the pickup to the underside of the string **A**. There is no precise distance at which this should be set. It's down to the pickup itself and, just as importantly, how you want to hear the sound balance between the two or three pickups. A rough guide for full-size humbuckers is to go for a gap of around 2.5mm (³⁄₃₂″) on the treble and bass sides of the neck and bridge pickups.

• Plug in your guitar and check the output balance of the pickups. If the neck humbucker dominates then screw it down further into the guitar body, away from the strings **B**. Some pickup makers such as Seymour Duncan offer "calibrated" sets of pickups. Because there is more string movement the further you move from the bridge, the strings' sound output will be greater over the neck pickup than over the bridge pickup. This can be compensated for by altering the pickup's output. So as a guide Duncan recommend setting a calibrated set of Duncan humbuckers at 1.6mm (¹⁄₁₆″) on the treble side and 3.2mm (⅛″) on the bass-side (top of pickup to underside of string).

• For single-coils you can go for a similar distance of 2.5mm (³⁄₃₂″) on the treble side and slightly more, around 3 to 3.5mm (⅛″ to ⁹⁄₆₄″), on the bass side **C**. With a Strat (again, unless you're using a calibrated pickup set)

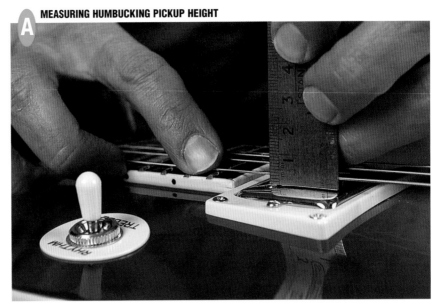

A MEASURING HUMBUCKING PICKUP HEIGHT

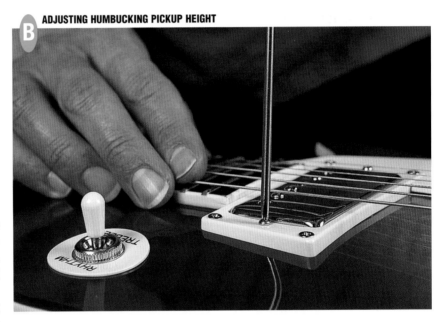

B ADJUSTING HUMBUCKING PICKUP HEIGHT

C MEASURING SINGLE-COIL PICKUP HEIGHT

D ADJUSTING SINGLE-COIL PICKUP HEIGHT

ADJUSTING HUMBUCKING PICKUP'S POLEPIECE HEIGHT

USING POT/SWITCH CLEANER

SPRAYING CLEANER INTO POT'S HOLE

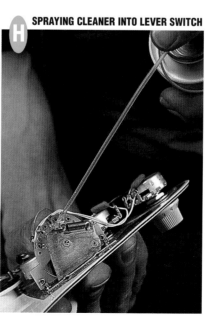

SPRAYING CLEANER INTO LEVER SWITCH

you may want to screw further down into the guitar the neck pickup **D** and, to a lesser extent, the middle pickup. Be prepared to sacrifice output – by lowering the pickup – especially on the bass side of the neck pickup to avoid the magnetic string-pull that can distort the strings' vibrational pattern, and create a double-note effect which can hinder accurate tuning.

POLEPIECE HEIGHT

Humbuckers (and some single-coils) have one or two rows of adjustable polepieces. Once you've set the pickup's overall height you can adjust these to compensate for both the radius of the fingerboard and the strings as well as their differing volumes caused by varying diameters and whether they're wound or plain types. Start off with the polepieces virtually flush with the top of the pickup.

Play your guitar amplified, preferably with a relatively clean amp tone, and compare the string outputs up and down the neck – and, obviously, one pickup at a time. You may find that the wound D-string is a little quiet compared to the A, so with the appropriate tool – usually either a flat-blade screwdriver or hexagonal Allen key – you can raise the polepiece slightly **E**. Note that you should avoid raising the top E polepiece too far as you could easily catch the string on it, with nasty results. Instead, use that string as your reference and reduce the height, if necessary, on the polepieces for the B- and G-strings.

CLEANING POTS & SWITCHES

Even brand new guitars can suffer from scratchy-sounding pots and selector switches (especially the Fender-style lever switch). Plug your guitar into your amp and continually rotate or activate the scratchy pot or switch. Does the scratching become reduced? If it does, all you need is an aerosol can of pot and switch cleaner such as Servisol **F**.

Expose the controls of your guitar and spray the cleaner into the small hole at the front of the pot **G** or into the lever switch **H**. Again, plug your guitar in and quickly rotate the pot or move the switch. You may need a couple of goes at this before the scratchiness is gone. If the pot still sounds scratchy or clicks, replacement is advised. On some guitars you may need to remove the control knobs and the pot itself to clean it. Overleaf we show how to remove knobs and access pots.

REMOVING KNOBS & ACCESSING POTS

• Inspect the knob to see if there is a grub-screw holding it to the pot. If there is, undo it with Allen key or screwdriver.

• Most guitars have push-on knobs, so try lifting the knob by hand.

• If the knob is too tight to move by hand, proceed as follows and with care. On Les Paul-style guitars, a tip passed on by UK maker Phil Norsworthy is to wrap a cloth tightly around the knob and gently pull it upwards while gripping the knob with your finger **I**. If it still won't budge, seek pro advice. *Do not* try to lever it with a screwdriver as it's easy to crack the knob or, worse, to damage the front of your guitar. On Strat-style guitars the less brittle plastic knobs do not crack so easily – but usually they sit lower on the guitar so you can't get a cloth around them. Here you can protect the pickguard with an old plastic credit card and, using a small flat-blade screwdriver, carefully and gently lever upwards **J**. (*Don't turn* the screwdriver: this will mark the bottom edge of the knob.) The key here is to slowly rotate the knob as you lever upwards. Once you've moved the knob up a little, wrap the cloth around it; you should be able to pull it off.

• With the knob removed, undo the pot's fixing washer with the correct-size box spanner **K**. The pot can then be moved, without unsoldering, to allow enough space to clean it. Be careful not to disturb the wiring.

• Sometimes pots work loose and rotate, but re-securing the control is easy. Remove the control knob as described and tighten the fixing nut with the box spanner, holding the pot itself to stop it rotating. Box-spanners are also very handy for tightening the fixing nuts of the output socket (jack) and the tuners – a job for which you should never use pliers.

• Lever switches are easily removed and/or secured using the two fixing screws at either end of the switch.

• A Gibson-style toggle switch has a ribbed circular nut to secure it onto the guitar. This is tricky to tighten and/or loosen as there is no "correct" commonly-available tool for the job. (Stewart-MacDonald's Guitar Shop Supply offer an appropriate Toggle Switch Wrench **L** but it's a specialist repairer's tool.) British luthier Sid Poole offers the following advice. "Before I got the Toggle Switch Wrench I dreaded this job. It's all too easy to damage either the nut itself, the plastic rhythm/lead ring, or the guitar's finish. So I suggest that you

protect the rhythm/lead ring with masking tape, and then use a pair of pliers held *very carefully* upright to slowly move the nut. You'll probably need to stop the switch rotating by holding it with a pair of snipe-nosed pliers from the rear of the guitar (obviously with the coverplate removed). It's a tricky job." For further protection you can wrap some masking tape around the tips of the pliers. *Never* attempt to over-tighten this nut. Above all, this apparently simple operation could damage your guitar, and so it really is a job for the pros.

Unless any component needs replacing, your existing electrics should now be in top condition. It's only at this point that you should consider whether you need a new pickup or maybe want to alter your guitar's wiring.

CLOTH-GRIP FOR KNOB REMOVAL
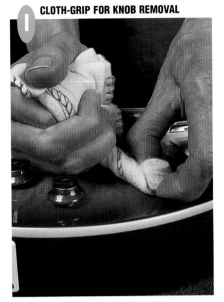

LEVERING KNOB FROM SHAFT
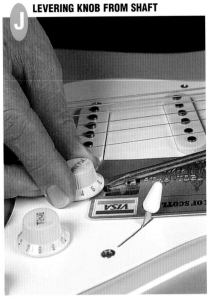

USING BOX SPANNER ON POT WASHER
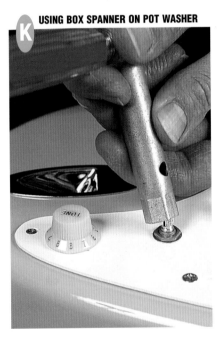

SPECIALIST TOGGLE SWITCH WRENCH

ELECTRICS HEALTH CHECK

• Check that the guitar's pickup heights are approximately correct.

• Check that each pickup and the selector switch is working.

• Check that each volume and tone control (plus any coil-splits) are working, and if any sound "scratchy".

• Check that the switches, pots and output socket are firmly fixed.

• Precisely set the heights of pickups and/or polepieces.

• Clean pots and switches if required.

• If necessary remove control knobs and tighten the fixing nuts of the pots and of the output socket (jack).

REASONS TO RETROFIT

There are four primary reasons for considering pickup replacement. First, your pickup may simply have stopped working. Uncovered pickups such as open-coiled humbuckers and Telecaster bridge pickups are susceptible to moisture penetration (beer, sweat, tears etc) which can lead to corrosion of the delicate pickup coil windings and shorting of the pickup. One answer is to have the pickup rewound, a service that should be considerably cheaper than investing in a new unit.

Second, and a more common occurrence on new and old guitars alike, is that your pickup(s) may squeal, or be "microphonic". These problems have a variety of causes depending on the type of guitar. Covered humbuckers – currently making quite a comeback – can squeal at high volumes. Often this is because the pickup has not been fully wax-saturated (although original-style PAF humbuckers are like this by design). Another reason is that the cover or pickup mounting may vibrate and cause microphonic feedback. Invariably the problem is magnified when you're using a high-gain, high-volume set-up. The options are to get your pickup properly waxed and maybe take specialist advice on the pickup mounting, or to fit a new pickup.

The third reason for considering pickup replacement is to do with a pickup's original design. Fender Strat and Tele pickups and Gibson's P90 are single-coil types. This means that they are susceptible to both low-cycle mains hum and higher-pitched hum and interference from fluorescent and stage lights and computer monitors. If the hum bothers you and/or the rest of your band, the cure is to replace the offending pickup(s) with humbucking replacements.

Finally, and perhaps most commonly of all, you might feel that your pickup is a weak link in your sound chain and you simply fancy a tonal change. Kent Armstrong reckons this is the main reason. EMG: "It's probably the least expensive and most direct way to change your tone. Most people get pretty comfortable with their guitar, so it's the quickest way to upgrade it." Seymour Duncan concur that players often look for a tone from their guitar that is not always provided by its stock pickups. "That's obvious," Duncan admit, "but many players are searching for a dream. They want to play and sound like their idol or someone they aspire to. Changing pickups helps further that dream."

PICKUP CONSIDERATIONS

Before we look at what a pickup can do, you need equally to be aware of what it can't do. As we've already discussed, an electric guitar can still be considered as an "acoustic". The combination of the guitar's design, materials, hardware, strings and set-up all contribute to that "acoustic" tone. The pickup then takes that inherent sound and sends it off to your amplifier. While no one is denying that the

Seymour Duncan and DiMarzio lead the market in retrofit pickups. Both produce excellent catalogues with tone descriptions, and offer a trial period to check out a pickup: if you're not satisfied, swap it for another. Seymour Duncan have recently issued three CDs ("Strats", "Teles" and "Humbuckers") which give examples of pickups in action.

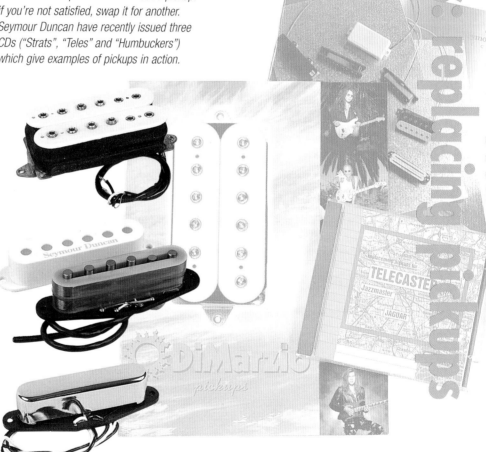

pickup forms a major part of your sound chain – and of course most pickup makers reckon it's the major part – it should not affect the acoustic performance of the guitar. Ideally the pickup should take the "information" – the strings' vibration – and ferry it as effectively as possible to your amplifier. So before you start pointing a finger at your pickup, make sure you've followed the instructions so far to adjust your guitar to its best potential. That includes fitting new strings – and always using a good-quality guitar lead (cord).

CHOOSING A PICKUP

For most of us, choosing a new pickup is always a risk. The only way to know if the new pickup is exactly what you need is to buy it, fit it and sound-test it through your own set-up. The best way to minimise the possibility of a mistaken purchase is to do some homework.

First you need to establish what it is that you don't like about your existing tone – assuming of course that you're happy with

your amp, FX and guitar. "That's the key," say Seymour Duncan, "Figure out why the existing pickup isn't happening for you. Does the bridge pickup in your Strat sound too thin? You have to identify the problem. Then you have to work out what you need: better harmonics, chunkier power chords? Think about your guitar and amp. What is the body and neck wood? Do you use a clean tone or melt-down metal? Then you can ask a dealer or repairman a specific question. 'I want a better sound from my Strat' is too vague, but, 'I want to beef up the bridge pickup on my alder-body maple-neck Strat which I use through a Fender Princeton amp to play blues' is what we need."

"Ideally you should test before you buy," say Kent Armstrong. "But that's the problem: you can't try everything. Talk to other players who have played them, and get some advice."

Both Seymour Duncan and DiMarzio provide tone charts in their product catalogues, comparing output (high or low) and bass, midrange and treble tone. A high-output pickup will drive a valve (tube) amp into overdrive more easily than a lower-powered pickup. The down-side is that you can often loose dynamics: there will be less distinction between light and heavily picked notes and the sound will be more compressed. You should be familiar with bass, midrange and treble from your hi-fi, but the electric guitar is really all about midrange. A classic Les Paul tone, for example, has a strong lower midrange helping to create its notorious thickness, but with enough upper midrange bite to cut through. But a classic Strat pickup will have less pronounced midrange, resulting in a "flatter", more acoustic tone. It'll also have plenty of upper-mids and highs for its classic sparkle.

Artist endorsements can help your choice too. All the big three companies – Seymour Duncan, DiMarzio and EMG – list in their catalogues many players and the set-ups they use, and this will at least give you some idea of the stylistic application of a certain pickup. "There are too many brands out there," say EMG, "and you can't hear them all. We'd suggest looking at your favourite players, finding out what they play and then taking a listen." For example, if you're after a vintage tone from your Les Paul you shouldn't buy a DiMarzio Evolution humbucker designed for Steve Vai, but go for their more classic-sounding PAF model. "As far as we're concerned," say EMG, "if an artist uses our pickups, it's their choice. They found them: it has nothing to do with us."

But in the end you're going to have to buy a pickup and live with it. If it's not 100 per cent right for you, at least by following the company's various comparative tone/output information it will be easier to fine-tune your future choice. These charts would tell you, for example, that if you'd purchased a DiMarzio Super Distortion humbucker but found it too aggressive sounding, then a DiMarzio PAF with its close approximation of the original Gibson PAF might be a better choice.

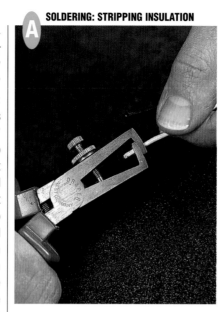

A SOLDERING: STRIPPING INSULATION

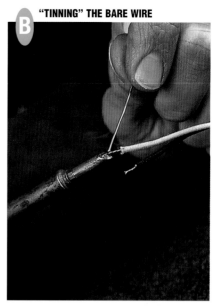

B "TINNING" THE BARE WIRE

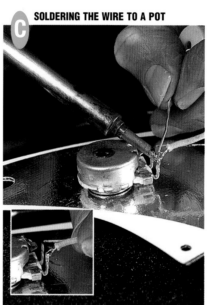

C SOLDERING THE WIRE TO A POT

D A COOLING WIRE KEPT IN PLACE

E USING A CROCODILE CLIP AS A HEAT-ABSORBING "HEAT SINK"

HOW TO SOLDER

Soldering is a process used to join electrical components and wires securely. If you want to fit your own pickup and maybe try some wiring mods you'll have to learn how to solder. It's much easier than learning to read music!

You'll need a small-tipped soldering iron, and it's worth buying a stand for it too. Small irons (25 watts) are fine for small connections but a more powerful iron (40 watts) is necessary for heavier jobs like soldering earth (ground) wires to the back of pots.

First you need to have your iron in good working order. If it's a new iron you'll need to tin the copper tip. If it hasn't been used for a while, clean the tip with fine to medium abrasive paper. Heat up the iron and place your solder (use a 60/40 rosin-core type) on the tip. Let the solder flow over the tip, then wipe off any excess with a damp – not wet – rag or sponge. Keeping your tip conditioned in this way is essential for good soldering. Periodically wipe the tip with a damp cloth. Some soldering-iron stands have a small sponge that can be dampened and used to wipe the iron tip. When your tip becomes blackened with use, re-clean it occasionally and re-tin it as previously described. Good preparation is the key to good soldering.

Having disassembled your guitar so you can access the relevant parts to be soldered, always cover the surface of your guitar with a cloth to stop splatters of solder marking the finish. Make sure you're clear on exactly what you are wiring where. Draw out the existing circuit before your start work, and then draw your modifications. That way you can always return the guitar to "stock". Clearly label these sketches and keep them for future reference.

• Most wires you'll be soldering have plastic or cloth insulation. Strip off about 3mm to 5mm (⅛″ to ³⁄₁₆″) with proper wire-strippers Ⓐ. If the core wire is multi-strand, twist it so it becomes solid. To "tin" the wire, apply heat from the iron to the bare end of the wire then touch the bare end with your solder which should flow over the exposed metal Ⓑ. You don't want too much solder. If a large blob transfers itself to the tip of the wire, re-heat and wipe off excess with a damp cloth. Note that a helpful addition to your soldering kit is a desoldering pump, or "solder sucker". Its spring-loaded piston is held over a fluid solder joint; when released it sucks away any excess solder. It's especially handy for working on mini-toggle switches (see Tools & Techniques p17).

• Wherever you can, make a mechanical joint before you solder the wire to the component. For example, pass the tinned wired halfway through a lug on a pot and bend it back on itself with a small pair of pliers. This will help secure the wire prior to soldering.

• Place the iron on the joint. Leave for a few seconds to heat. You'll get a feel for this, depending on exactly what you're soldering and how powerful the iron is you're using. Then place the solder on the joint and let it flow Ⓒ. Remove the solder, then the iron, and let the joint cool. Don't blow on it. When it's cool, just tug on the wire to make sure the joint is secure. It should look shiny and chrome-like. A grey and dull appearance is a sure sign of a "dry" joint where the solder hasn't flowed – and neither will the electrical signal – so you'll need to resolder the connection.

• Securing wires to the back of the pots is always difficult. First prepare the pot. Rough the soldering surface with medium abrasive paper or score with the edge of a blade-tip screwdriver, wipe off any debris (with a cloth, not your greasy finger) and tin the back of the pot, creating a small dome of solder. Lay your tinned wire in place, hold it, and heat it with the tip of your iron. Apply solder. When the solder has flowed place the tip of a small screwdriver or probe on the wire Ⓓ, to keep it in place while the solder cools, and remove the iron.

• Wire insulation can melt if subjected to excess heat, while small components like capacitors can be damaged. So when soldering a capacitor, for example, use a crocodile clip as an absorbing "heat sink" by placing it on the relevant "leg" between the component and the joint Ⓔ. Don't forget: soldering practice makes perfect.

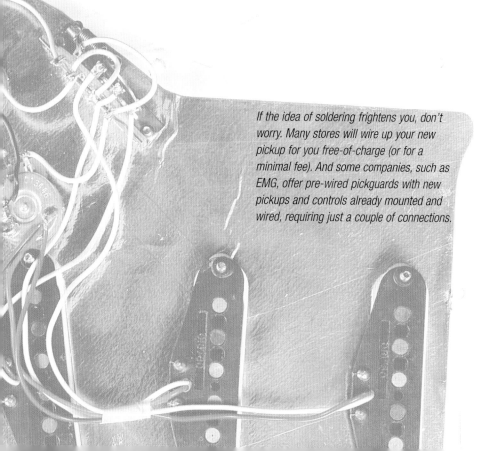

If the idea of soldering frightens you, don't worry. Many stores will wire up your new pickup for you free-of-charge (or for a minimal fee). And some companies, such as EMG, offer pre-wired pickguards with new pickups and controls already mounted and wired, requiring just a couple of connections.

new pickup, check to see if the old height-adjustment screws fit the threaded lugs on the new pickup. Don't force them – just use your fingers to see if they'll turn in the thread. If they do, then go ahead and use them. If not, use the screws supplied.

3 Mount the new pickup in the old mounting ring. This is actually quite a tricky job. Insert one screw at a time through the ring, place the spring over the screw, and grip the pickup and mounting ring so that the end of the screw is held over the thread on the pickup's mounting lug. With a small cross-head or slot-head screwdriver (depending on the screw type) carefully turn the screw so that it bites into the pickup's thread (pictured left). Don't force it – you may damage the thread. The new height adjustment screws will probably be too long and you'll need a pair of heavy duty cutters to trim them to length. But first screw the pickup down into the ring to match the distance you measured originally. Replace the pickup in the guitar. Does it sit flush on the body, or are those screws stopping it? If necessary cut them to length with heavy-duty cutters a few millimetres (about $\frac{1}{16}''$ or so) past the back face of the mounting lugs.

4 Carefully thread the hook-up wire through the hole that connects the pickup cavity to the rear control cavity (pictured left), wrapping masking tape around any loose wires. Replace the pickup into the guitar, securing it with just two of the mounting-ring screws at diagonally opposite corners. At this stage don't cut the pickup wire to length. Strip, tin and re-solder the live wire to the relevant volume control and the earth wire to the back of the pot. If the pickups have four-conductor wiring make sure you follow the supplied wiring diagram and join the remaining two conductors (for series linkage) as described.

• Rub the tip of a screwdriver on the pickup polepieces to check that the new pickup is working and check all the control functions (as described earlier in Fitting A Single-coil Pickup p70). Fit a set of new strings (see p20-22) and tune your guitar to pitch. Set the height of the new pickup. Refit the remaining mounting-ring screws and refit the control cavity backplate. Only after fully sound-testing your guitar should you cut the pickup wires to correct length and re-solder the hot connection using a mechanical joint.

REPLACING A TELE BRIDGE PICKUP

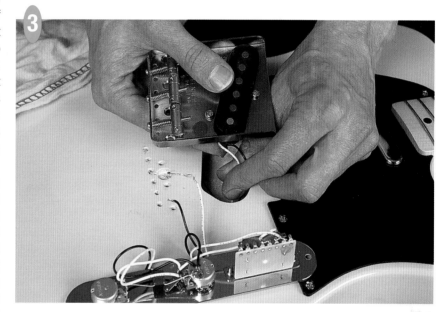

Electrics: replacing pickups

REPLACING A HUMBUCKER

Working on a set-neck Les Paul-style guitar is less easy than a bolt-on. Also, we're showing the bridge pickup: if you're replacing the neck humbucker you'll have to remove the bridge pickup too so you can thread the neck pickup's hook-up wire through the bridge pickup's cavity into the rear control cavity.

1 Before you start, make sure the existing pickup heights are about right (see pXX). Measure and note down the distance from the top of the mounting ring to the top of the humbucker(s) you're replacing. Remove your strings (or alternatively put a capo at the first fret, slacken off the strings, and remove the tailpiece and bridge). Remove the rear control cavity's backplate. Unsolder the live pickup wire from the correct control (pictured), and unsolder the earth (ground) wire from the back of the pot. (It may not be clear which pickup wire goes where. Don't worry, just partially remove the pickup as described in the next step and gently pull on its hook-up wire to trace which pot it's soldered to. Put two of the mounting-ring screws back, then unsolder the relevant wires.)

2 Turn the guitar over and remove the pickup by unscrewing the four cross-head screws that hold the pickup mounting ring. Carefully pull the pickup, still held in its mounting ring, away from the guitar (pictured). Unscrew the two pickup height-adjustment screws carefully. Make sure you don't lose the two long springs as new ones are not always supplied. Before you mount the

PHASED AND CONFUSED?

When two humbucking or single-coil pickups are combined (with the switch in positions two or four on a Strat, or the switch in the middle position on a Les Paul or Telecaster), they will be either "in-phase" or "out-of-phase".

The main cause of pickups being out-of-phase is incorrect magnet polarity. When pickups are out-of-phase the resulting mixed sound will be thin (in other words, bass-light) and "strangled" or overly nasal sounding. You may like this sound, especially for high-gain grungy tones or clean reggae/funk/country tones. On the

other hand, you may not like the sound of out-of-phase pickups. Standard single-coil pickups are easy to cure. All you have to do is simply swap over the live and earth connections where they connect to the pickup switch.

Curing an out-of-phase humbucker with just one live wire and earth is more difficult because, unlike a standard single-coil, the earth wire is connected to the metal baseplate and the cover (if fitted). Swapping these two around will result in hum.

Telecasters can be especially problematic because the earth wire of the bridge pickup is connected to its own

grounding plate, and the neck pickup's earth wire connects to the metal pickup cover. The simplest solution is to swap the connections for the neck pickup – but you must rewire the neck pickup's cover to the "new" earth output, which is a job for a pro or a specialist pickup repairer.

If you're thinking of mixing different brands of pickups on your guitar, always make sure that the humbucker has three or preferably four conductor wires and a separate earth wire (for more about this, see Replacing a Humbucker, above). This way any phase problems for standard pickup linkages can be solved.

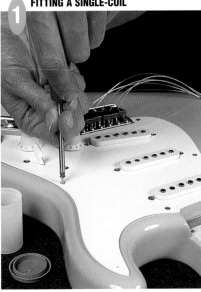

FITTING A SINGLE-COIL

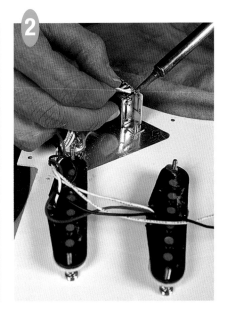

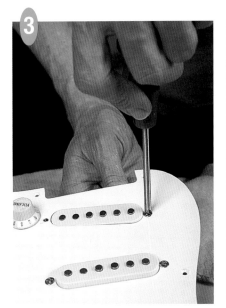

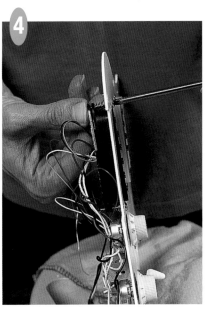

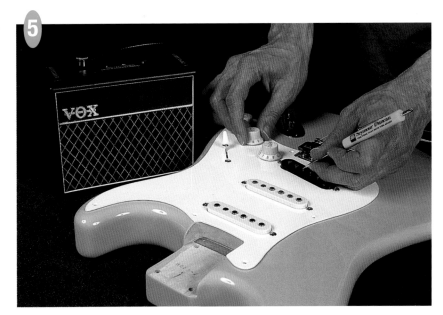

FITTING A SINGLE-COIL PICKUP

Many current Fender Strats are perfect guitars for electrics modification. Under the pickguard there's a large oblong pickup cavity rather than the three separate pickup routs (plus channel) found on a vintage-spec Strat. The oblong rout means that fitting humbuckers is easy, and new pickguards are readily available as spares. The fact that you can remove the neck with the strings still on also makes life easier: the pickguard is accessible, and you can quickly re-assemble the guitar to try it out.

1 Remove the neck (see p31/32) and put it aside; unscrew the pickguard (pictured).

2 Carefully turn over the pickguard and rest it securely on the covered guitar body. Trace the wires from the pickup that you're replacing: one should be already soldered to the five-way switch, the other to the back of a volume pot. Sketch the circuit, then unsolder the relevant wires (pictured) by heating the joints and pulling the wires free.

3 Unscrew the old pickup (pictured), taking care to keep the springs or rubber tubing that goes over the fixing-screw between the pickup and the pickguard.

4 Load in the new pickup using the supplied screws and the old springs (pictured) or rubber tubing.

5 Strip and tin the ends of the pickup wires, but at this stage don't cut them to length. When you've sound-tested your new pickup and are sure that's the one you want, then you can go back into the guitar and tidy up your wiring. Solder the new pickup wires in place but don't at this stage worry about a mechanical fixing as there's a 50/50 chance that your new single-coil with be out-of-phase with your existing pickup (see Phased And Confused p71). Before you re-assemble your guitar, plug it into your amp (keep the volume low) and lightly rub (don't tap) the tip of a screwdriver on the pickup polepieces (pictured). You'll hear a sound through your amp if the new pickup is working. Then check that the selector switch and the volume and tone controls are all working correctly. Re-assemble your guitar.

• Make sure you really test out your new pickup (and/or any wiring mods) before you finally decide it's right. When you've given it the thumbs-up, open up your guitar and tidily cut, re-strip and re-solder the connections, using mechanical joints if possible.

REPLACING A TELE BRIDGE PICKUP

1 Unlike any other electric, the Telecaster and its derivatives has a bridge pickup that is mounted within the bridge's baseplate. It's held with three screws, and under the pickup is a grounding plate (pictured). The combination of these design features contributes to the Tele's unique tone – but can also add to microphonic squeal, especially if the pickup's windings are not properly wax-potted and if there's any movement of the pickup and/or the bridgeplate. In order to replace a Tele bridge pickup, first remove the strings. You have little choice with this, because to access the bridge pickup you'll have to remove the bridge itself. Measure the height of the pickup from the face of the bridgeplate, on both treble and bass sides. Make a note of these dimensions.

2 Unscrew the control plate and sketch the wiring layout. Unsolder the pickup's hook-up wires (pictured). As with the humbucker replacement, if you're unsure which wires are which, then remove the bridge's baseplate by undoing the four mounting screws and gently pull on the two hook-up wires to trace one to the three-way lever switch and one to the back of a pot.

3 With the hook-up wires unsoldered, remove the bridge's baseplate and the pickup (pictured), undoing the four baseplate screws first if you haven't already. Replace the control plate and place the guitar to one side.

4 Remove the pickup from the bridge's baseplate and mount the new pickup (pictured). Some players and makers insist on replacing the pickup's mounting springs with small pieces of plastic tubing. Others simply believe that you should replace the springs. Either way, the key is to make sure that the springs or tubing are very tight and firm, and that once the pickup is mounted there's virtually no movement within the baseplate. Set the pickup approximately to the original position. Strip and tin the hook-up wires.

5 Undo the control plate and thread the hook-up wires into the control cavity. Solder them to the correct positions: the live wire goes to the three-way lever switch, the earth (ground) wire to the back of a pot. Place both the control plate and the bridgeplate in position and scratch-test the pickup to check that it's working. Replace all the screws (pictured) and re-string the guitar. Tune up, and then set the pickup height (see p64).

WIRING MODIFICATIONS

Now that we've covered the basic aspects relating to your guitar's electrics, you can use this Wiring Modifications section should you need to replace any components or upgrade and modify your guitar.

REPLACING COMPONENTS

When you replace any component there are some basic rules.
• Sketch out your guitar's existing circuitry *before* you start.
• Unsolder the old component to be replaced.
• Remove the old component and install the new.
• Re-solder the new component and scratch-test before re-assembling guitar.

Semi-solid guitars such as Gibson's ES-335 are very fashionable at the time of writing, but are among the trickiest when it comes to working on the electrics. The problem is that this type of guitar has no backplate, so to service the parts or replace the pickups you must remove the pots and switches through the pickup cavities or f-holes. For this reason we suggest you take your semi to a professional.

Volume and tone pots ❶ ❷ ❷ₐ *In most cases you can replace volume and tone pots with standard splined-shaft pots of the required value and taper (see p63). Before you install the new pot, however, check that the control knob actually fits onto the new pot. The slotted, splined shaft can be slightly widened*

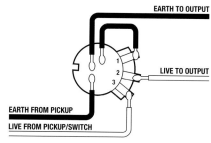

❶ *Standard volume*

by carefully opening the tip of the shaft with a flat-blade screw driver, or narrowed by slightly compressing the tip of the shaft with a pair of pliers. But be warned: the tips of these shafts are surprisingly fragile. The tools and techniques for un-mounting a pot are the same as those shown for cleaning (see p66); here, of course, we completely unsolder the old component and load in the new one.

Output jack socket (jack) ❸ *The majority of electric guitars use a mono output jack socket (jack). It simply has one connection for the live (hot) output and another for the earth (ground) output. Take care to replace the jack socket with one of a similar size, especially on Stratocaster-style guitars where the jack socket sits under the separate "dished" mounting plate. A standard "chassis" type socket is recommended in this situation.*

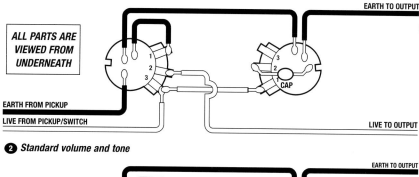

ALL PARTS ARE VIEWED FROM UNDERNEATH

❷ *Standard volume and tone*

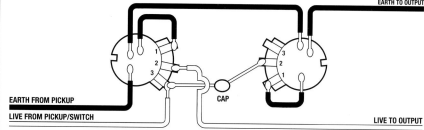

❷ₐ *Alternative volume and tone*

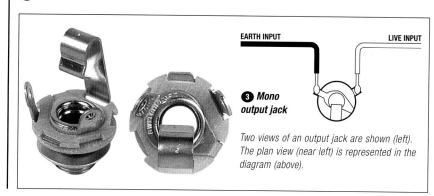

❸ *Mono output jack*

Two views of an output jack are shown (left). The plan view (near left) is represented in the diagram (above).

PICKUP SELECTOR SWITCHES

Most Fender-style guitars and many, many others use either a three-position lever switch (for two-pickup guitars) or a five-position lever switch (for three-pickup guitars) to select the pickups. The other industry standard switch is the three-position toggle or leaf-style switch used on Gibson-style guitars primarily with two pickups.

Three- and five-position lever switches You'll encounter a number of different types within two basic categories: "open" and "closed". A standard US-made open type is preferred, and is featured here **4**. Measure the distance between the centres of the two mounting holes, which can differ, to check that your new switch will fit.

For three- or five-position switches, the mechanics are the same. It's a "two-pole" switch – it has two circuits that are switched simultaneously. We refer to

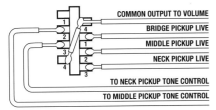

COMMON OUTPUT TO VOLUME
BRIDGE PICKUP LIVE
MIDDLE PICKUP LIVE
NECK PICKUP LIVE
TO NECK PICKUP TONE CONTROL
TO MIDDLE PICKUP TONE CONTROL

4 *US five-position lever switch*

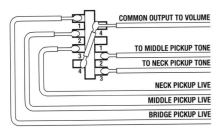

COMMON OUTPUT TO VOLUME
TO MIDDLE PICKUP TONE
TO NECK PICKUP TONE
NECK PICKUP LIVE
MIDDLE PICKUP LIVE
BRIDGE PICKUP LIVE

4a *US five-position lever switch (Fender)*
Typically, Fender wire their five-position switch the reverse of **4**. Either way will work.

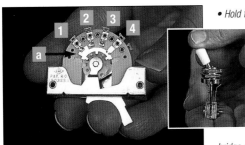

Parts of five-position lever switch.

these poles or circuits as "sides", simply because of the physical construction of the switch. On each side there are four connection tags: three input/output tags and one common tag.

If your replacement switch doesn't come with a wiring diagram, you can visually check the switch.

• Hold the switch upside down in front of you with the non-spring side facing you and the selection lever all the way to the right. When the switch is wired in, this position (position one) will select the Stratocaster's bridge pickup.

• Below the row of connection tags you'll see (photo below left) that the large square lug (a) is in contact with one of those four connection tags. Sketch out the switch and mark this tag as number one. Move the lever to the furthest position to the left (position five) and make a note of which connection tag the square lug is now in contact with, and mark this as number three; this is where you connect the neck pickup. Mark the tag between these two as number two; this will be your middle pickup connection. (Remember, originally a Strat had a three-way switch – you couldn't combine the pickups. The five-way switch simply joins connection tags one and two and connection tags two and three to create the famous mixed-pickup Strat sounds.)

• The fourth connection is the common connection. Mark this as number four.

• Return the lever all the way to the right. Now turn the switch so the spring side is facing you and mark on your sketch which connection the square lug is now in contact with. Mark this as number one. Do the same for all the switch positions as above and mark them, finally marking the common connection. Now, when the switch is in position on the pickguard you can follow your sketch to determine which wires go to which connection tags.

Three-position toggle switch **5** Like the three- and five-position lever switches, the three-position toggle or leaf-style switch comes in a number of styles and sizes. (Again, not least because you can see which connection tag does what, go for an "open" type as opposed to the square "closed" type.) Typically, a longer switch is used in a Les Paul and a shorter type in a thinner-bodied guitar like an SG. The switch has two input connections (for each pickup) and two output connections which must be joined on the switch to provide the common output. A fifth connection – usually in the centre of the switch – connects to earth (ground). Again, you can visually check which contact does what, as follows.

• Hold the switch upright so that the toggle moves from left to right with the outer (or both sets) of connection tags facing you.

• Place the toggle to the left (the up position, which on a Les Paul selects the neck pickup) and you will see that the right pair of contacts are opened (pictured) so you wire the neck pickup to the outer connection tag of the left pair, and the bridge pickup to the outer tag of the right pair. With the toggle in the centre position you'll see that both pairs of contacts are joined – that's how you get both pickups on together.

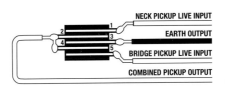

NECK PICKUP LIVE INPUT
EARTH OUTPUT
BRIDGE PICKUP LIVE INPUT
COMBINED PICKUP OUTPUT

5 *Three-position toggle switch*

BASIC WIRING MODIFICATIONS

If your pickups and controls are working properly, you can use the following simple wiring mods to alter the way in which the controls affect your pickup's output.

Treble bleed network This is a simple modification that can be applied to any volume control. By placing a small capacitor (typically .001mf) between the input (connection tag one) and output (tag two) of the pot, as you turn down the volume control you'll retain the high end of your tone **6**. When wiring in the capacitor you're advised to use a heat-sink (crocodile clip) as you solder each leg.

Some companies prefer the effect of an additional resistor wired (in parallel with the capacitor) between the same two tags **6a**. The reason is that you may find the capacitor alone makes the sound too thin with the volume control reduced. "The additional resistor tends to restore the lower (bass) end when the control is turned down," reckons DiMarzio's Steve Blucher. The normal value for this resistor is 150k ohms, but Blucher thinks this allows too much bass resistance. "The bigger the resistor's value, the less you're limiting bass. I don't use anything below 300k ohms."

Tone control capacitors Another subtle change you can make is by experimenting with different-value capacitors in your tone control(s). In this circuit the capacitor shunts off the treble frequencies to earth (ground), in other words the opposite of the treble bleed network. Standard values are .047mf, .02mf and .01mf. Remember, the value of the capacitor determines the frequency point above which the treble roll-off takes place. The smaller the capacitor's value, the higher the frequency point and the less effect the capacitor will have in terms of cutting the treble as the control is wound down (see p63). So, if you find your tone control sounds too dark – and it uses a .047mf capacitor – try a .02mf or a .01mf. Conversely, if it doesn't sound dark enough and you're using a .02 or .01, try a .047. On a guitar with two tone controls, like a Les Paul or Strat, you can use different values.

Strat tone controls Typically a Strat is wired so that the first tone control (the centre of the three controls) affects the neck pickup, and the second tone control (furthest from the bridge pickup) works on the middle pickup; there is no tone control for the bridge pickup **7**. Some players like to change this, and it's easy to

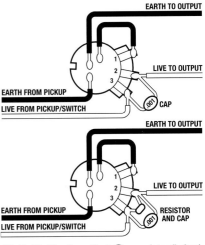

EARTH TO OUTPUT
LIVE TO OUTPUT
EARTH FROM PICKUP
LIVE FROM PICKUP/SWITCH
CAP

EARTH TO OUTPUT
LIVE TO OUTPUT
EARTH FROM PICKUP
LIVE FROM PICKUP/SWITCH
RESISTOR AND CAP

6 *Treble bleed cap (top)* **6a** *+ resistor (below)*

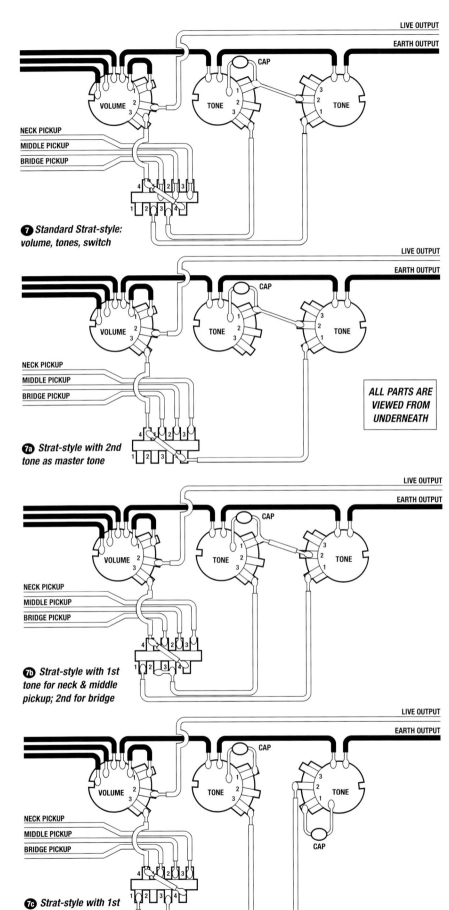

LIVE OUTPUT
EARTH OUTPUT

VOLUME
TONE
CAP
TONE

NECK PICKUP
MIDDLE PICKUP
BRIDGE PICKUP

7 *Standard Strat-style: volume, tones, switch*

LIVE OUTPUT
EARTH OUTPUT

VOLUME
TONE
CAP
TONE

NECK PICKUP
MIDDLE PICKUP
BRIDGE PICKUP

ALL PARTS ARE VIEWED FROM UNDERNEATH

7a *Strat-style with 2nd tone as master tone*

LIVE OUTPUT
EARTH OUTPUT

VOLUME
TONE
CAP
TONE

NECK PICKUP
MIDDLE PICKUP
BRIDGE PICKUP

7b *Strat-style with 1st tone for neck & middle pickup; 2nd for bridge*

LIVE OUTPUT
EARTH OUTPUT

VOLUME
TONE
CAP
TONE

NECK PICKUP
MIDDLE PICKUP
BRIDGE PICKUP

CAP

7c *Strat-style with 1st tone for neck pickup; 2nd for bridge pickup*

do. The late Rory Gallagher, for example, wired his Strat so that only the second control functioned, but as a master tone control for all three pickups **7a**.

Alternatively, you could use the first tone control for both the neck and middle pickups and the second tone control for the bridge pickup **7b**. Another popular option is to use the first tone control for the neck pickup and the second tone control for the bridge pickup, leaving the middle pickup without a tone control **7c**. This gives tone control for the often-used soloing pickups (neck and bridge) while the "rhythm" settings (the Strat's combined pickup tones) benefit from the full treble of the middle pickup. Try this with different tone capacitor values.

Pickup switches Fitting a new full-sized humbucking pickup to your guitar, so long as the pickup has four hot conductors and a separate ground, opens up a host of switching options. First, we've shown the standard wiring for a four-conductor humbucker in series operation **8** and parallel operation **8a**. Please

CONDUCTOR TIME

Virtually all of the major-brand retrofit pickups come with four-conductor (plus earth) hook-up wire. If you're swapping brands and/or plan to add some wiring options, this format is recommended. The four conductors come from each end – the start and finish – of the two wound coils: I & II. To help you we've included a colour-code comparison chart here of three major brands of passive pickups. However, all pickups should come with clear instructions – follow those first and use our chart for reference.

		DiMarzio	Duncan	WD/Sky
COIL I	**start (A)**	green	green	red
	finish (B)	white	red	black
COIL II	**start (C)**	red	black	green
	finish (D)	black	white	white

(Note: the bare wire is always wired to earth.)

Series humbucker: conductor A) goes to earth; B) and D) are joined; C) is live. But if pickup is out-of-phase, reverse the position of conductors A) and C). If you reverse the phase of the pickup by swapping conductors A) and C) you will voice the opposite coils to those indicated below.
Parallel humbucker: A) and D) joined to earth; B) and C) joined to live.
Coil I single-coil: A) earth; C) live; B) and D) go to live.
Coil II single-coil: A) earth; C) live; B) and D) go to earth.

Note: Coil I usually refers to the humbucker's screw-coil and Coil II to the slug-coil.

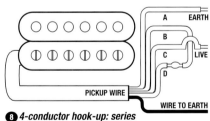

A EARTH
B
C LIVE
D

PICKUP WIRE
WIRE TO EARTH

8 *4-conductor hook-up: series*

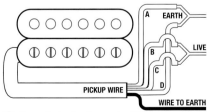

A EARTH
B
LIVE
C
D

PICKUP WIRE
WIRE TO EARTH

8a *4-conductor hook-up: parallel*

note that the four conductors are labelled a, b, c, and d, which relate to the Conductor Time chart (see p75). There are, however, numerous ways to switch between these standard wirings – and also to add more sounds – simply by installing an additional switch (or two). We'll consider two main types: the mini-toggle switch, and the pull/push switched pot.

Two-position (on/on) single pole, double throw (SPDT) mini-toggle switch (pictured above) This can be used to coil-split a humbucker from its standard series humbucking mode to either one of the humbucker's single coils **9** **9a**. You could achieve a similar effect using the spare lug on a tone control **9b**, or utilise the unused side of a lever switch (see Steve's Wizardry, opposite page).

SPDT mini-toggle switch (left); underside view of DPDT (above left) and SPDT (above right)

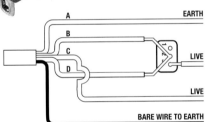

9 *SPDT series/Coil I*

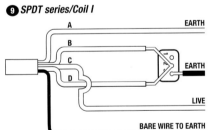

9a *SPDT series/Coil II*

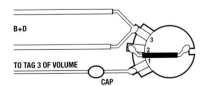

9b *Tone coil-split. Instead of using a switch (**9** or **9a**) to split a humbucker, use a tone control. Turning tone full on results in coil split. Wire rest of circuit as **2**: the cap replaces wire from tag 3 of volume to tag 1 of tone.*

FITTING A MINI-TOGGLE SWITCH

This means drilling a hole in your guitar's pickguard – we do not recommend fitting this type of switch on a guitar without a pickguard. You could place the mini-toggle, for example, between the tone controls of a Strat. Here's what you do.

• Select the position for the switch – check there's room for the switch in relation to the other components and the body's control cavity – and mark with a pencil.
• Remove all the pickups and pots.
• Make a small indentation at your pencil mark with a centre punch or sharp point. This will stop the drill bit slipping off position when you start drilling.
• Using a G-clamp or two, securely clamp the pickguard to a piece of flat waste timber or board.
• Select a 6.4mm (¼") drill bit. Wrap masking tape around the end of the bit so that it is beyond the thickness of the pickguard but less than the combined thickness of the pickguard and your waste board. This will tell you when to stop drilling.
• With a hand-drill (or an electric drill on a *slow*

Drilling carefully through the pickguard, which is clamped onto a piece of waste board.

speed) place the tip of the drill in the marked indentation and slowly and carefully drill through the pickguard (pictured above). Load in the existing components and the new switch.

Two-position (on/on) double pole, double throw (DPDT) mini-toggle switch (pictured left) This is like two SPDT switches ganged together. If you want to coil-spilt two humbuckers simultaneously, use either of the SPDT diagrams (left, below) and assign one side of the switch for the neck pickup and the other for the bridge pickup.

But this switch also has many other uses. For example, it can be used to switch the phase relationship between two pickups, or to switch between the way the humbucker is wired, either in series (standard), or in parallel that will produce a brighter tonal characteristic with a lower output that is noise-cancelling.

Three-position (on/on/on) double pole, double throw (DPDT) mini-toggle switch This can be used to offer series, single-coil and parallel wiring of one humbucker **10a**.

Pull/push switched pots If you don't want to alter your guitar in any way you can still achieve pickup switching with a "pull/push" switched pot. This combined DPDT switch and pot can replace either a volume or tone control (or both) and will not alter the look of your guitar. This option is essential for any guitar that will be affected in value by any modification. If you're going to add a switch, this is the one we'd recommend. All the diagrams for the on/on DPDT mini-toggle switches also apply to the pull/push switched pot.

Fitting a pull/push pot is the same as fitting either a tone or volume pot, except that you must take into account the extra room needed in the control cavity. Also, extra care must be taken when you fit the control knob; should you need to remove the control knob at a later stage it's all to easy to pull off the knob and the innards of the pull/push switch. You have been warned!

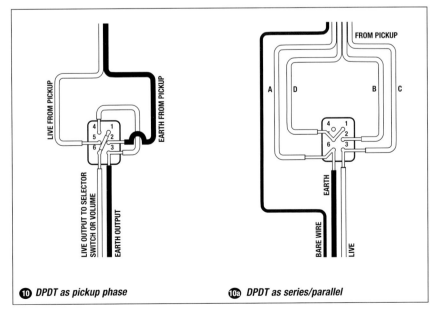

10 *DPDT as pickup phase*   **10a** *DPDT as series/parallel*

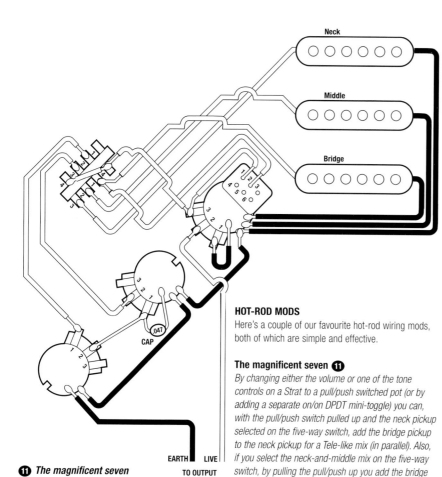

Neck

Middle

Bridge

.047
CAP

EARTH LIVE
TO OUTPUT

11 *The magnificent seven*

HOT-ROD MODS

Here's a couple of our favourite hot-rod wiring mods, both of which are simple and effective.

The magnificent seven **11**

By changing either the volume or one of the tone controls on a Strat to a pull/push switched pot (or by adding a separate on/on DPDT mini-toggle) you can, with the pull/push switch pulled up and the neck pickup selected on the five-way switch, add the bridge pickup to the neck pickup for a Tele-like mix (in parallel). Also, if you select the neck-and-middle mix on the five-way switch, by pulling the pull/push up you add the bridge pickup for all three pickups on. This expands the Strat's five pickup selections to a magnificent seven.

GET SCREENED?

Electric guitars are susceptible to picking up hum and buzz, which in extreme cases can be very annoying. This of course is one reason why the humbucker was invented. A humbucking pickup by design uses electromagnetic screening to reduce low-cycle hum. But additional electrostatic screening or shielding may be necessary to reduce the higher-frequency noise generated by stage lights and computer monitors.

To this end some guitars, including Fender's American Standard, for example, have their control and pickup cavities painted with carbon shielding paint while the back of their pickguards have a layer of conductive aluminium foil. (The American Standard Strat's middle pickup is reverse-wound with reverse polarity so that positions two and four on its five-way switch are noise-cancelling.) However, while this electrostatic screening may help, it is difficult to fully screen single-coil pickups (a primary source of hum). So if hum bothers you, in reality you'd be well advised to change your pickups for humbucking or noise-cancelling types.

A professional can advise you on hum problems. Using screened cable between components (some manufactures do, others don't) will not increase the problem. With any wiring modification, always check that the earth connections run continuously from the pickups to the switches and controls and then on to the output socket (jack). Always check that the earth wire from the bridge is connected to earth (the back of a pot). You can visually check this, or use a multimeter.

ALL PARTS ARE VIEWED FROM UNDERNEATH

A
B
C
D
Neck

Middle

C
D
B
A
Bridge

VOLUME
500k

TONE
250k   .02
CAP

LIVE

TO OUTPUT

EARTH

12 *Steve's Wizardry*

Steve's Wizardry **12**

Designed for Steve Vai in 1986 by DiMarzio's Steve Blucher, this wiring is found on numerous Ibanez guitars that have a humbucker at neck and bridge, plus a single-coil in the middle position. Because the set-up uses a master volume and master tone on one side of a standard five-way lever switch, the other side can be used to automatically coil-split the neck and bridge humbuckers. (You can use the same principle to automatically split the humbucker on a guitar that is fitted with a humbucker at the bridge plus one or two single-coils.)

Blucher's wiring gives us: position one, neck humbucker; position two, bridge-facing single-coil of the neck humbucker plus middle single-coil; position three, middle single-coil; position four, neck-facing single-coil of the bridge humbucker plus middle single-coil; position five, bridge humbucker.

On Steve's original diagram the middle single-coil is reverse-wound with opposite polarity compared to the bridge-facing single-coil of the neck humbucker and the neck-facing single-coil of the bridge humbucker. Therefore all positions except three on the five-way switch are noise-cancelling. Note that because this circuit was specifically designed for DiMarzio pickups, you may experience problems with the noise-cancelling effect and the phase relationship in positions two and four. However, physically reversing one humbucker in its mounting ring should create the correct phase relationship and noise-cancelling effect.

CLASSIC ELECTRIC GUITAR SCHEMATICS

Included on this page are three benchmark guitar wiring layouts for standard Stratocaster (left), modern Telecaster (below left), and Gibson Les Paul (below).

While some of the various models and interpretations of the Stratocaster, Telecaster and Les Paul that have been marketed over the years and that are being sold today will necessarily feature non-standard schematics, those shown here should provide a basic working reference. Use these as starting points when you are planning maintenance or modifications to your instrument.

However it is worth bearing in mind that before you start working on *your* guitar, you should make a detailed sketch out its own particular wiring. Also please note that, for clarity, in each of the wiring layouts shown here we have not included the earth wire that will run from the bridge/vibrato to any earth point (the back of a pot).

ALL PARTS ARE VIEWED FROM UNDERNEATH

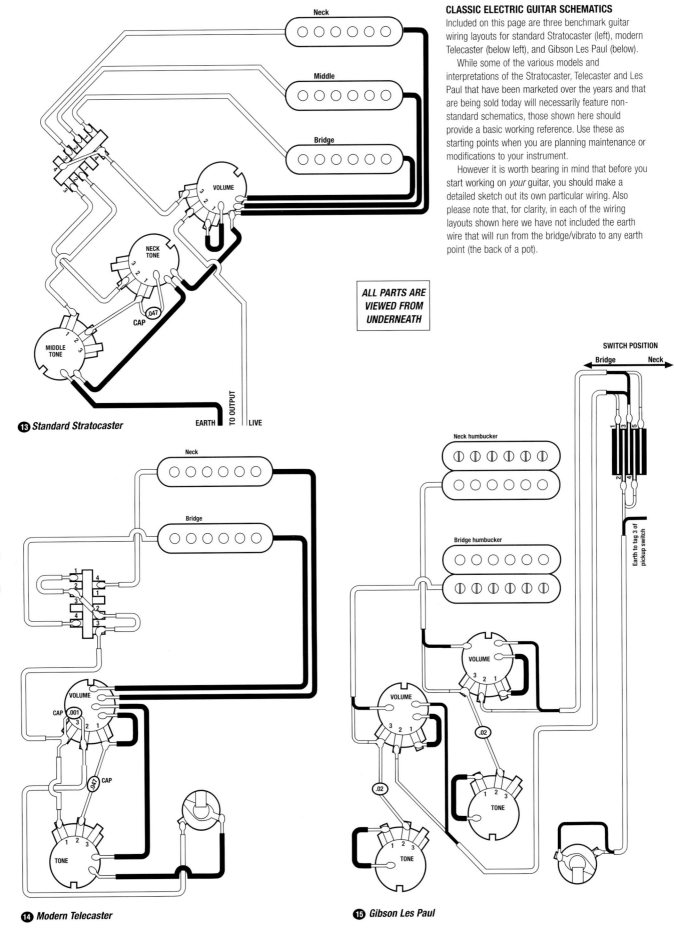

13 *Standard Stratocaster*

14 *Modern Telecaster*

15 *Gibson Les Paul*

CARE & CLEANING: BODY AND NECK

"Plastic" finishes The majority of modern electric guitars are finished with a high-gloss "plastic" finish such as polyester or polyurethane. Some major brands (Gibson, for example) still use nitro-cellulose-based finishes, though due to a combination of factors, not least air-pollution regulations and drying time, cellulose finishes are rarely used today – apart from on some high-end "Custom Shop" guitars.

These finishes are applied from a spray gun, then flattened and polished up to a mirror-like gloss on a high-speed buffing wheel. This is a time-consuming process requiring numerous coats of finish, and for many production instruments actually forms a major part of the manufacturing time. Apart from looking good, the finish protects the guitar from dirt and grease which, once it gets into the wood-grain, is hard to remove. The finish also seals the wood from moisture penetration which can cause numerous problems related to the timber's stability.

Most manufacturers simply suggest you polish up your guitar body (and other finished wood parts like the back of the neck) with a "guitar polish", usually wax-based, and with or without silicone. The problem with products using silicone is that any future refinishing and/or repairs will be made even more difficult. So if you use a guitar polish, make sure it's silicone-free.

The best way to clean your guitar is with a dry, lint-free cloth or duster *immediately* after playing. This will remove all sweat and grease before it has time to solidify and form a harder-to-remove residue. Remove stubborn build-ups with a *barely* damp cloth. Never, *never* use a wet cloth. Always rub the guitar immediately after with a totally dry and clean cloth.

If your guitar is looking a little shabby and dirty, your best bet is a proprietary *mild* finish restorer – a fine buffing/burnishing cream. Don't use car products: they're too coarse. Manson's Finish Restorer or one of the Mirror Glaze polishes are ideal.

• Remove the strings and apply a little buffing cream to a dry, soft cloth and work onto the guitar's surface in small circular areas. The buffing cream will remove dirt, grease and small scratches. Keep rubbing on the same small area for a high sheen, then move to an adjacent area and apply more. Finally, polish all over the finish with a new, dry, soft cloth without any buffing cream.

Oil finishes These involve a light oil being applied directly to the wood, and have a varying reputation among makers, repairers and store owners. Although there is credibility to the belief that the thinner the body finish the better the tone, a thin oil-finish is very susceptible to penetration from dirt and moisture. Apart from any tone considerations, many players simply like the look and feel, especially on a neck, of the natural wood.

An oil finish requires very regular maintenance – and even then, an oil-finished maple neck and fingerboard will inevitably look dirty very quickly. An important rule is that you must always wipe an oil finish after playing. Music Man, for example, recommend occasional cleaning with lemon-oil applied sparingly with a soft cloth. You may notice, especially if you sweat a lot, that the back of the neck begins to feel "furry" where your sweat has caused the grain to rise. Flatten this with very fine abrasive paper (or 0000-grade wirewool) and then a little furniture wax on a soft cloth.

Occasionally you may need to re-oil the wood before waxing with a tung-based oil like Danish oil. Certainly you can achieve a very good-feeling neck with this regular maintenance programme, but an oil finish will rarely give you the protection of a proper finish that seals the wood parts. So some manufacturers now use a very light matt finish which simulates the look of an oil finish, but has better moisture protection and needs less maintenance.

FINGERBOARD

The majority of fingerboards are unfinished rosewood or ebony. Most maple fingerboards have a finish much like the body and can be cleaned in the same fashion. However, be careful with old, fragile and cracked finishes where bare wood is showing; you won't get these clean, and if the discoloration really bothers you then consult a pro.

For bare rosewood and ebony fingerboards you need an *occasional* application of a lemon-oil-based fingerboard cleaner. (Several companies offer such a fingerboard cleaner which has a lemon-oil base. Make sure you always use a preparation intended for fingerboard cleaning.) Here's what to do.

• Remove the strings and apply a small amount of lemon-oil to a soft cloth or paper towel and rub it into the fingerboard. (It's worth noting that some makers discourage the use of lemon-oil or indeed any oil-based preparation for fear that it could have a softening effect on the fingerboard. However, used sparingly and occasionally, it's unlikely to do any damage.)
• Leave the oil to penetrate for a few minutes, then rub it off with a clean cloth or paper towel which should remove most of the grime and leave the board looking brand new. Grime can build up right next to the fret, so work some lemon-oil into these areas on a cloth wrapped around your fingernail (a plectrum will work if your nails are too short). Stephen Delft's Boogie Juice is a fingerboard cleaner with a felt tip; this makes it ideal to remove hard-to-access fingerboard grime. Always use lemon-oil sparingly and occasionally; again, your best line of defence against fingerboard grime is to rub down the strings and fingerboard after every playing session with a dry, soft cloth.

STRINGS

There are various string-cleaning and lubrication products: Manson's String Cleaner works well to remove grime from strings.

• Apply a little string-cleaner directly to the strings, then wrap a piece of soft cloth or paper towel around and under each string, and move it quickly up and down the entire length. (Any cleaner residue that goes onto the fingerboard itself can be cleaned off in the same fashion, and actually helps to remove fingerboard grime.) Fast Fret is another string preparation that many swear by. It won't make you play faster (only practice does that) but a little application on the plain strings helps to keep them in good condition. You should ideally aim to avoid any "lubricating" string preparations with an oil base, especially on a wound string. These can actually attract dirt in between the windings (wrap) of wound strings, and so make them go dead more quickly.

HARDWARE & PARTS

The metal parts on your guitar are typically plated with nickel, chrome, or gold. Sweat (or any moisture) is the major enemy here – again, rubbing down with a soft cloth immediately after playing is your best defence. Bridge saddles often become caked with grime and can corrode (and in some cases rust) after years of playing and non-maintenance. Here's how to clean them.

• First remove the strings, then the saddles, but be very careful with the small intonation- and height-adjustment screws. If these screws are fitted tight they may have corroded, so remove the whole bridge assembly and – away from your guitar – spray on some penetrating oil. (Remember, you should never spray oil anywhere near your guitar.)
• Give the penetrating oil some time to do its job and then (without excessive force) carefully try again to turn the problem screw. If it's still tight, leave the part to soak overnight. If it is still stuck fast you may have to consider replacement or professional help. For mildly corroded saddles, a good rub with penetrating oil will not only clean off any debris but in the short-term will stop any further corrosion.

If the plating has become dulled (or if the metal part is unplated brass or aluminium) a proprietary metal polish will restore most of the sheen – and even the mild buffing cream we used on the finish works very well too. Black hardware was popular a few years back. In some cases this was little more than thin black paint which wears off quickly; proper black-coloured plating or black chroming on hardware should have the same lifespan as standard plating methods, and should be cleaned accordingly.

Plated pickup covers should just be cleaned with a dry cloth; you really don't want any "wet" polishing compound getting into the pickup. But if you make sure the cloth that you've used to apply metal polish elsewhere is dry, then go ahead and use that – but don't apply any more polish.

Plastic pickguards, knobs and pickup covers can also be simply wiped down with a dry cloth, or cleaned and polished, if necessary, with the fine buffing cream. However, you don't want to get any cream in the pickup or control components, so remove the plastic pickup covers from the pickups and remove any other components from the pickguard before you clean it. Uncovered pickups should be cleaned with just a dry cloth (or one that's slightly dampened if the grime is stubborn – but make sure you rub any slight moisture away immediately with a dry cloth).

Above all, protect your guitar with a good quality case. A gig-bag is fine for personal transportation but in a car boot (trunk), or in a van in the proximity of amps and drums, it won't offer the protection your guitar deserves. And never expose your guitar to extremes of temperature (or humidity). Never leave it close to a radiator, or in a vehicle overnight. Your guitar is a tool to make music with. Treat it with respect and it'll last a lifetime... or more.

Alternative terms are shown (in brackets) following the key word.

acoustic Related to sound or hearing. An acoustic musical instrument is one that is capable of generating sound without electrical amplification.

action *43* Often used to describe just the height of the strings above the tops of the frets; thus "high action", "low action", "buzz-free action" etc. In fact, action refers to the entire playing feel of a given instrument; thus "good action", "easy action" etc.

active (active electronics, active circuit) Circuitry in some guitars that boosts signal and/or widens tonal range with necessary additional (usually battery) powering. Refers generally to a pickup or circuit that incorporates a pre-amp. See **pre-amp.**

Alnico Magnet material used for pickups: an alloy of aluminium, nickel, and cobalt.

amplifier Electrical circuit designed to increase a signal; usually, an audio system for boosting sound before transmission to a loudspeaker.

archtop Guitar with arched body top formed by carving or pressing. Usually refers to hollow-body or semi-acoustic instruments; thus "archtop jazz guitar".

attenuate Reduce in strength.

backlash Any "give" in a tuner's operation where the string-post does not immediately move when the tuner button is turned.

backplate Panel fitted over cavity in rear of guitar body allowing access to pots and wiring or vibrato springs.

ball-end Metal retainer wound onto the end of guitar string, used to secure it to the anchor point at the bridge.

bar pickup see **blade pickup**

binding Protective and decorative strip(s) added to edges of the body and/or fingerboard and/or headstock of some guitars.

blade pickup (bar pickup) Pickup (either humbucker or single-coil) that uses a long single blade polepiece per coil, rather than the more usual individual polepieces per string.

bobbin *56, 59* Frame around which pickup coils are wound.

bolt-on neck *24, 25, 31-33* Neck-to-body joint originally popularised by Fender – and actually most often secured by screws.

bound see **binding**

bout Outward curves of guitar body above (upper bout) and below (lower bout) guitar's waist.

bridge Unit on guitar body that holds the saddle(s). Sometimes also incorporates anchor point for strings.
function *38*
"hardtail" *26*
Leo Quan Badass *38, 39*
Les Paul Junior *26*
PRS *26, 39*
saddle see **saddle**
Stratocaster *26*
Telecaster *39, 44, 49*
trapeze *39*
Tune-o-matic see **Tune-o-matic bridge**
types *38-39*
vibrato bridges see **vibrato**
Wilkinson GB-100 *39*
wrapover see **wrapover bridge**

bridge pickup Pickup placed nearest the bridge.

bridgeplate On electric guitars: baseplate on to which bridge components are mounted. (On acoustic guitars: reinforcing hardwood plate under bridge.)

bullet Describes appearance of truss-rod adjustment nut at headstock on Fender-style guitars.

camber see **radius**

capacitor (cap) *63* Electrical component that accumulates electric charge. Within an electric guitar tone control, for example, it's used to filter high frequencies to earth, making the sound progressively darker as the control is turned down.

capo (capo tasto, capo dastro) Movable device which can be fitted over the fingerboard behind any given fret, shortening the string length and therefore raising the strings' pitches.

cavity Hollowed-out area in solidbody guitar for controls and switches: thus "control cavity".

cellulose see **nitro-cellulose**

centre block Solid wooden block running through inside of semi-acoustic guitar's body.

chamfer Bevel/slope to body edges.

choking *37* String colliding with a higher fret as it's played and/or bent.

cleaning *65, 79*

coil(s) Insulated wire wound around bobbin(s) in a pickup.

coil-split *59* Usually describes a method to cut out one coil of a humbucking pickup giving a slightly lower output and cleaner more single-coil-like sound. Also known, incorrectly, as coil-tap.

coil-tap (tapped pickup) *62* Pickup coil which has two or more live leads exiting at different percentages of the total wind in order to provide multiple output levels and tones. Not to be confused with coil-split.

compensation (scale length) *26* Small distance added to each string's speaking length to make the guitar play in-tune. This additional string length compensates for the sharpening effect that occurs when the strings are pressed down onto the fingerboard.

compound radius see **radius**

conductor wires *75* Wires attached to the start and finish of a pickup coil which take the output signal to the controls. A four-conductor humbucker, for example, actually has five output wires: four conductor wires (labelled A, B, C and D in this book; see p75) and a fifth (bare) wire which comes from the pickup's grounding plate and/or cover and must always be connected to earth.

conical radius see **radius**

contoured body Gentle curving of solid guitar body, aiding player comfort.

control(s) Knobs and switch levers situated on the outside of guitar that activate the function of electric components usually mounted through the pickguard or from the back of the body. See also **pickup switch.**
knob *63, 66*
Les Paul *57, 78*
screening *77*
Stratocaster *57-58, 74-75, 78*
Telecaster *78*
tone *57, 63, 73, 74*
treble bleed *74*
volume *57, 63, 73*

course Usually means a pair of strings running together but tuned apart, most often in unison or an octave apart, as on a 12-string guitar.

cross-head screw/screwdriver Screw with two slots in a cross shape in its head. Screwdriver with a cross-shaped point to fit such a screw (sometimes known as a Phillips type).

cutaway Curve into body near neck joint, aiding player's access to high frets. A guitar can have two ("double", "equal", "offset") cutaways or one ("single") cutaway. Sharp ("florentine") or round ("venetian") describe the shape of the horn formed by the cutaway.

damping Deadening of a sound, especially by stopping the vibration of a string with the palm of the hand, etc.

DC resistance "Direct current" resistance: a measurement (in ohms) often quoted in pickup specs to give an indication of relative output.

dead string length Portion of the string situated beyond the nut and behind the saddle.

distortion Signal degradation caused by the overloading of audio systems. Often used deliberately to create a harsher, grittier sound.

dive-bomb see **down-bend**

dog-ear Nickname for some P90 pickups, derived from the shape of the mounting lugs on cover.

double-locking vibrato see **locking vibrato**

down-bend Downward shift in the strings' pitch using a vibrato. In extreme cases this is known as "dive-bombing".

DPDT switch Double-pole double-throw miniature switch.

dropped headstock (pointed headstock, droopy headstock) Long, down-pointing headstock popularised on 1980s superstrats.

earth (also known as ground, especially in the US) Connection between an electrical circuit or device and the ground. A common neutral reference point in an electrical circuit. All electrical components (and shielding) within a guitar (and amplifiers, signal processors etc) must be linked to earth as the guitar's pickups and electrics are susceptible to noise interference (see Get Screened p77). See **shielding.**

electric A term simply applied to any electric guitar, in other words one used in conjunction with an amplifier.

electro-acoustic (electro) Acoustic guitar with built-in pickup, usually of piezo-electric type. The guitar usually has a built-in pre-amp including volume and tone controls.

electronic tuner Typically battery-powered unit that displays and enables accurate tuning of an instrument to standard concert pitch.

equalisation (EQ) Active tone control that works by emphasising or de-emphasising specific frequency bands.

farad Measure of electrical capacitance that (for electric guitar capacitors) is usually quoted in microfarads (mf or µf)

feedback Howling noise produced by leakage of the output of an amplification system back into its input, typically a guitar's pickup(s).

f-hole Soundhole of approximately "f" shape on some hollow-body and semi-acoustic guitars.

fine-tuners Set of tuners that tunes strings to very fine degrees, usually as fitted to a locking vibrato or bridge.

fingerboard (fretboard, board) *36-37, 79* Playing surface of the guitar that holds the frets. It can be simply the front of the neck itself, or a separate thin board glued to the neck.

finish Protective and decorative covering on an instrument's wood parts, typically the guitar's body, the back of its neck, and the headstock.

five-way switch (five-position switch) *62, 74, 78* Selector that offers five options, for example the five pickup combinations on a Strat-style guitar.

fixed bridge Non-vibrato bridge.

fixed neck see **glued neck**

flat-blade screwdriver see **slot-head screwdriver**

flat pick see **plectrum**

floating bridge Type of bridge that is not fixed permanently to the guitar's top, but which is held in place by string tension (most often on older or old-style hollow-body guitars).

floating pickup Pickup not fixed permanently to the guitar's top, but mounted on a separate pickguard or to the end of the fingerboard (on some hollow-body electric guitars).

floating vibrato Vibrato unit (such as the Floyd Rose or Wilkinson type) that "floats" above the surface of the body.

frequency Number of cycles of a vibration occurring per unit of time: the perceived pitch of a sound. See **Hertz**.

fret(s) Metal strips positioned on the fingerboard of a guitar (or sometimes directly into the face of the solid neck) to enable the player to stop the strings and produce specific notes.

fretboard see **fingerboard**

fretwire Wire from which individual frets are cut.

gauge Outer diameter of a string, universally measured in thousandths of an inch (.009", .042" etc). Strings are supplied in particular gauges and/or in sets of matched gauges. Fretwire is also offered in different gauges, or sizes.

glued neck (glued-in neck, set neck, fixed neck) *24, 25, 33* Type of neck/body joint popularised by Gibson which permanently glues the two main components together.

ground see **earth**

ground wire Wire that is typically connected from vibrato, bridge, tailpiece, switch, pickup cover or grounding plate etc to earth (ground).

grounding plate Metal baseplate of pickup connected to earth.

hardware Any separate components (non-electrical) fitted to the guitar: bridge, tuners, strap buttons, etc.

harmonic Ringing, high-pitched note produced by touching (rather than fretting) strategic point on the string while it is plucked.

headstock Portion at the end of the neck where the strings attach to the tuners. "Six-a-side" type (Fender-style) has all six tuners on one side of the headstock. "Three-a-side" type (Gibson-style) has three tuners on one side and three the other.

Hertz (Hz) Unit of frequency measurement. One Hertz equals one cycle per second (see **frequency**).

hook-up wire Connecting wire (live or earth) used to make connection from pickup to pots, switches etc.

horn Pointed body shape formed by cutaway: thus left horn, right horn. See also **cutaway**.

hot In electrical connections, means live. Also used generally to mean powerful, as in "hot pickup".

hot-rodding Mod(ification).

humbucker pickup *56, 58, 59, 61, 64, 71-72, 75* Noise-cancelling twin-coil pickup. Typically the two coils have opposite magnetic polarity and are wired together electrically out-of-phase to produce a sound that we call in-phase. See **phase**.

impedance Measure of electrical resistance to the flow of alternating current. A few electric guitars/pickups have low-impedance circuits or pickups to match the inputs of recording equipment; the vast majority are high impedance. Impedance matching is important to avoid signal/tone loss.

inertia block see **sustain block**

inlay Decorative material cut and fitted into body, fingerboard, headstock etc.

insulation Plastic, cloth or tape wrapping (non-conductive) around an electrical wire to prevent wire(s) coming into contact with other components and shorting the circuit.

intonation State of a guitar so that it is as in-tune with itself as physically possible. This is usually dependent on setting the string's speaking length by adjusting the point at which the strings cross the bridge saddle, known as intonation adjustment. Some bridges

allow more adjustment, and therefore greater possibilities for accurate intonation, than others.

jack see **jack socket**

jackplate Mounting plate for the output jack socket (jack) that is usually screwed on to the body.

jack socket (jack) *57, 73* Mono or stereo connecting socket, usually 6.35mm (¼"), used to feed guitar's output signal to amplification.

knurled Serrated or cross-hatched patterning to provide grip on metal (or plastic) components; thus "knurled control knobs" (as fitted to a Telecaster-style guitar).

lacquer see **nitro-cellulose**

laminated A material joined together in layers; usually wood (bodies, necks) or plastic (pickguards).

leaf switch see **toggle switch**

lever switch *62* Type of pickup selector switch historically used by Fender, for example the five-way lever switch. A single, pivoted lever moves between contacts to direct the input-to-output path. See **pickup switch**, **selector**, **toggle switch**.

linear taper see **taper**

locking nut Unit that locks strings in place at the nut, usually with three locking bolts.

locking tuner *21, 22, 34, 53* Special tuner that locks the string to the string-post and thus aids string-loading.

locking vibrato *40, 41, 51* Type of vibrato system that locks strings at nut and saddles (hence also called "double-locking") to stabilise tuning.

logarithmic taper see **taper**

lower bout see **bout**

lug Protruding part or surface. On electrical components a lug (sometimes called a tag) allows a connection to be made, usually by soldering.

luthier Guitar maker.

machine head see **tuner**

magnetic pickup Transducer that uses coils of wire wound around a magnet. It converts string vibrations into electrical signals.

master volume/tone Control that affects all pickups equally.

microfarad see **farad**

microphonic Of a pickup: one that is inclined to squeal unpleasantly, usually due to incomplete wax saturation, loose coil windings, or insecure mountings that create microphonic feedback.

micro-tilt neck *31* Device built into some Fender (and other makers') neck-to-body joints allowing easier adjustment of neck pitch.

mod Short for modification; any change made to a guitar.

mounting ring Usually plastic unit within which a Gibson-style pickup is fitted to the guitar body.

multimeter *17*

neck *24-37*

neck pitch *31* Angle of a guitar's neck relative to the body face.

neckplate Single metal plate through which screws pass in order to achieve a bolt-on neck fixing (Fender-style). Some bolt-on neck-to-body joints use separate washers for each screw.

neck pickup Pickup placed nearest the neck.

neck pocket Rout, or recess, into which the neck fits on the body of a bolt-on neck guitar.

neck relief *28, 29, 30, 43* Small amount of concave bow in a neck (dipping in the middle) that can help to create a relatively buzz-free action.

nitro-cellulose (lacquer in the US) Type of finish originally used commonly in the 1950s/1960s but now rarely used on production guitars.

noise Any undesirable sound, such as mains hum or interference.

noise-cancelling pickup *59* Type of pickup with two coils wired together to cancel noise, often called humbucking. Any arrangement of pickups or coils that achieves this.

nut *26* Bone, metal or (now usually) synthetic slotted guide bar over which the strings pass to reach the tuners and which determines string height and spacing at the headstock end of neck.

nut lock see **locking nut**

ohm Unit of electrical resistance.

shielding (screening) Barrier to any outside electrical interference. Special paint or conductive foil in the control/pickup cavity to reduce electrical interference. See **earth**.

signal Transmitted electrical information, for example between control circuits, or guitar and amplifier, etc, usually by means of a connecting wire or lead (cord).

single-coil pickup *56, 58, 59, 65, 67, 70, 71, 75* Original pickup type with a single coil of wire wrapped around a magnet or magnets.

slab board (slab fingerboard) Fender type (originally circa 1959-62) in which the joint between the top of the neck and the base of the fingerboard is flat. Later this joint was curved.

slot-head screw/screwdriver Screw with a single slot in its head. Screwdriver with a flat, single blade (sometimes known as a flat-blade type).

slot-head tuner Tuner with a slot cut into the top of its string-post with a hole running down the centre of its string-post.

soap-bar Nickname for P90 pickup with a cover that has no mounting "ears". See **dog-ear**.

soldering *17, 68-69*

solid General term applied to any solidbody electric guitar.

soundhole Aperture in top of acoustic guitar's body that increases sound projection. Similar function to f-holes on hollow-body and semi-acoustic guitars.

SPDT switch Single-pole double-throw miniature switch.

speaking length Sounding length of the string: the part running from the nut down to the bridge saddle.

splined Grooved surface of potentiometer shaft to assist tight fitting of control knob.

spring claw *46, 47* Anchor point for vibrato springs in rear "vibrato cavity". Adjustment of the spring claw's two screws affects the position and potential travel of the vibrato.

stock State, irrespective of condition, of a guitar where everything is exactly as supplied new. Individual items on a guitar exactly as supplied new ("stock pickup", for example).

stop tailpiece see **stud tailpiece**

strap button Fixing point on body to attach a guitar-strap; usually two, on sides (or side and back) of guitar body.

string(s)
Bigsby *52*
buzz *28-29*
changing see loading (later)

cleaning *23, 79*
distances, 12th fret *32-33*
Floyd Rose *50-51*
gauge *23, 29, 43, 46, 48*
height *26, 31, 35, 43-45*
loading *20-22, 23, 50-51, 52*
retainer bar see **string-retainer bar**
stretching *22-23, 53*
tension *24-25, 26*
tinning *54*
tree see **string tree**
types *20*

string length see **scale length**

string-post Metal shaft on tuner with a hole or slot to receive the string and around which the string is wound.

string-retainer bar *51* Metal bar typically placed behind locking nut to seat strings over curved surface of locking nut prior to locking. Also occasionally used like a string tree to increase behind-the-nut string angle on guitars without nut locks.

string tree *25, 53* Small unit fitted to headstock that maintains downward string-tension at nut.

string winder Device to assist in the speedy winding of a string onto the tuner's string-post.

stud tailpiece (stop tailpiece) *38, 39, 44* Type of tailpiece fixed to solid or semi-acoustic guitar top, either as a single combined bridge/tailpiece unit, or as a unit separate from the bridge.

superstrat Updated Fender Stratocaster-inspired design popularised in the 1980s: it had more frets, deeper cutaways, changed pickups, and a high-performance (locking) vibrato.

sustain Length of time a string vibrates. Purposeful elongation of a musical sound, either by playing technique or electronic processing.

sustain block (inertia block) *46* Metal block situated under the bridgeplate of a floating vibrato (a vintage Fender type, for example) which, because the vibrato is not permanently fixed to the body, replaces the necessary body mass that is necessary to achieve sufficient string sustain.

system vibrato see **vibrato system**

tag see **lug**

tailpiece Unit on the guitar's body separate from the bridge that anchors the strings. (See also **stud tailpiece**.)

taper *63* Of a potentiometer: determines how smoothly the resistance is applied as the control is turned down. Most modern pots use a logarithmic taper as opposed to a linear taper.

tapped pickup see **coil-tap**

thinline Hollow-body electric guitar with especially narrow body depth; term coined originally by Gibson for their mid-1950s Byrdland model.

three-way switch (three-position switch) *62, 74* Selector switch that offers three options.

through-neck Neck that travels the complete length of guitar, usually with "wings" added to complete body shape.

timbre Distinctive tone quality, or "colour", of a sound.

tin To apply solder to a wire before making the actual solder joint.

toggle switch *18, 62, 74* Type of selector switch that "toggles" between a small number of options. Sometimes called a leaf switch.

tools *15-19*

top nut see **nut**

transducer Unit that converts one form of energy to another; the term is sometimes used generically for piezo-electric pickups, but applies to any type of pickup or, for example, loudspeaker. See **magnetic pickup**, **piezo pickup**.

treble-bleed cap Simple circuit where capacitor (sometimes with an additional resistor) is attached to volume control potentiometer and thus retains high frequencies when the volume control is turned down.

tremolo (tremolo arm, tremolo system, trem) Erroneous but much-used term for vibrato system. The musical definition is the rapid repetition of a note or notes. This is presumably where Fender got the name for their amplifier effect, which is a regular variation in the sound's volume. See **vibrato**.

truss-rod *28* Metal rod fitted inside neck, almost always adjustable; can be used to control a neck's relief.
adjustment *28, 29, 30*
box-section *28, 29*
dual-action *28*
Fender *29, 30*
Gibson *28, 30*
single-action *28, 29*

truss-rod cover Decorative plate covering truss rod's access hole, usually on headstock.

Tune-o-matic bridge Gibson-originated bridge that is adjustable for overall string height and for individual string intonation.

tuner Device that is usually fitted to a guitar's headstock and that alters a string's tension and pitch. Also called machine head or (archaically) tuning peg. See also **electronic tuner**.

tuner button Knob that the player moves to raise or lower a tuner's pitch.

tuning *23*

two-pole see **pole**

unwound string see **wound string**.

up-bend Upward shift in the strings' pitch brought about by using a vibrato.

upper bout see **bout**

urethane see **polyurethane**

vibrato (vibrato bridge, vibrato system, tremolo, tremolo arm, trem, wang bar, whammy) Bridge and/or tailpiece which alters the pitch of the strings when the attached arm is moved. Vibrato is the correct term because it means a regular variation in pitch.
arm position *54*
Bigsby *40, 41, 52*
Fender *40, 41, 45, 46-47, 54-55*
Fishman Powerbridge *42*
floating *47*
Floyd Rose *40, 41, 47, 50-51*
history *40*
Ibanez Lo-Pro *41-42*
Kauffman Vibrola *40*
locking see **locking vibrato**
PRS *42, 44*
tuning *51, 53*
types *41-42*
Wilkinson *40, 42, 45, 47*

vibrato system System comprising locking vibrato bridge unit, friction-reducing nut and locking tuners.

waist In-curved shape near middle of guitar body, usually its narrowest point.

wiring diagrams
five-way switch *74*
humbucker *75*
jack (socket) *73*
"magnificent seven" *77*
mini-toggle *76*
pickup phase *76*
series/parallel *75, 76*
"Steve's wizardry" *77*
Stratocaster *75, 77*
tone *73, 74*
output *73*
tone coil-split *76*
treble bleed *74*
volume *73*

wound strings Typically the three lowest-pitch strings fitted to the guitar, with metal windings around a metal core. See also **plain strings**.

wrapover bridge Unit where strings are secured by wrapping them around a curved bar.

zero fret Extra fret placed in front of the nut. It provides the start of the string's speaking length and creates the string height at the headstock end of the fingerboard. In this instance the nut is simply used to determine string spacing. Used by some manufacturers to even out the tone between the open string and the fretted string.

Acknowledgements

Special thanks to my musical Mum and craftsman Dad, Ali, Lauren and Lucy... and to Ron Wood, Dan Armstrong and Tony Zemaitis for getting me hooked!

This book would most certainly not have been possible without the experience, time and assistance of Bill Puplett (guitar repairer to the stars); the care and attention (and total disregard to the rants of this author) of Tony Bacon, Nigel Osborne, Sally Stockwell, Phil Richardson and Miki Slingsby at Balafon; and the understanding folk at *The Guitar Magazine* (UK). Thanks also to Tony Bacon for the Electric Guitar Styles section.

Thanks must in addition go to the many **distributors**, **manufacturers** and also **individuals** who supplied info and/or guitars/parts for this book: Kent Armstrong (Rainbow Products); Dave Beeson (Saddle Singers); Phil Dearing; Nikki Donnelly (Arbiter/Fender); Chris Eccleshall; FCN Music; Simon Frazier-Clarke (Headstock/Ibanez); Dave Good (Elites Strings);Gordon-Smith Guitars; Martin Hartwell (Aria UK/Seymour Duncan, Gretsch/Gotoh); Jay Hostetler (Stewart MacDonald); Christine Kieffer (Rosetti/Epiphone); Mike Lewis (Fender USA); Manson's Guitar Shop; Jim Matthews; Barry Moorhouse (Elites Strings); Graham Noon (Akai/Jackson); Russell Prince (Elites Strings); Toni Rutherford (Akai/Jackson); Stentor Music; Peter West (Rainbow Products); Mike Westergaard.

The author would also like to thank all the **guitar/accessory makers** as well as the **repairers/technicians** who have given their time, help and advice: Kent Armstrong; Steve Blucher (DiMarzio); Charlie Chandler; Seymour Duncan; Hugh Manson; Doug Marhoffer (EMG); Phil Norsworthy; Sid Poole; Mark Pressling (Arbiter); Tim Shaw (Guild/Fender); Evan Skopp (Seymour Duncan); Danny Smith; Rob Turner (EMG).

And finally I'd like to thank all the **designers**, **guitar makers**, **repairers**, **journalists** and **wheeler-dealers**, who have over the years taken time to explain their craft, especially Paul Reed Smith, Ken Parker and Larry Fishman, Ned Steinberger, Trevor Wilkinson, Rob Green (Status Graphite), Doug Chandler, Jol Dantzig (Hamer Guitars), Max Kay, Hap Kuffner, Paul Day and many, many others.

Historical instruments

The photographs of instruments in the Electric Guitar Styles section (pages 6-14) come from the Balafon Image Archive. Guitars included were owned by the following at the time of photography, and we are most grateful for their help: Scot Arch (Les Paul Sunburst, Les Paul gold-top/humbuckers, Silver Jet); Chinery Collection (Les Paul Special, Stratocaster, 335); Keith Clark, Voltage (Rickenbacker Combo 400); Jennifer Cohen (White Falcon); Country Music Hall of Fame (Bigsby); Gruhn Guitars (Telecaster, Les Paul gold-top/P90s); JHS (Jackson); David Noble (Les Paul Junior); Alan Rogan (Crestwood, Rickenbacker 12-string).

Illustrations

The step-by-step photography featured throughout this book was devised by Nigel Osborne and photographed by Miki Slingsby in the lavish and spacious surroundings of the Rosslyn Hill studio. The diagrams in the Reference section were electronically composed by Phil Richardson without alien intervention. Extra thanks should also go to the Buzzard, the Hawk, and Bill Bigsby.

Trademarks

Many of the individual products described in this book are identified by their trade names (Telecaster, Stratocaster, Les Paul, and so on) which are claimed as legally protected trademarks by the companies that manufacture and/or market these products. Rather than clutter the book with ™ symbols, we state here that we are simply using the names in an editorial fashion and that we do not intend to infringe any trademarks.

BIBLIOGRAPHY

Donald Brosnac *Guitar Electronics* (DM Music/Bold Strummer 1980)
Ralph Denyer *The Guitar Handbook* (Dorling Kindersley 1992)
Seymour Duncan *Guitar Tone Secrets Revealed* (video: Power Rock 1997)
Dan Erlewine *Guitar Player Repair Guide* (GPI Books 1994)
Melvyn Hiscox *Make Your Own Electric Guitar* (Blandford Press 1990)
Hideo Kamimoto *Complete Guitar Repair* (Oak Publications 1975)
Adrian Legg *Customising Your Electric Guitar* (Windmill Press 1981)
Tom Wheeler *The Guitar Book* (Macdonald Futura 1975)

Magazines consulted for research included: *The Guitar Magazine* (UK), *Guitar Player*, *Fender Frontline*, *Hamer Tone*, Stewart MacDonald's *Guitar Shop Supply* catalogues, *The Ground Wire* and pickup catalogues (Seymour Duncan).

"The first rule of all intelligent tinkering is to save all the parts."
Paul Ehrlich (German scientist)